PROFESSIONAL SKILLS FOR TRAINEE SOLICITORS

PROFESSIONAL SKILLS

FOR

TRAINEE SOLICITORS

Charles Brady

BA, LLM, Solicitor; Managing Director, Central Law Training

and

Gillian Parry

MA (Oxon), Solicitor; Training Manager, Central Law Training

Central Law Publishing

A division of Central Law Training Ltd

© *Central Law Training Ltd* 1992

Published by
Central Law Publishing
A division of Central Law Training Ltd
Centre City Tower
7 Hill Street
Birmingham B5 4UA

ISBN 1 85811 000 9

Printed in Great Britain by BPCC Wheatons Ltd, Exeter

CONTENTS

NOTE: In order to avoid the tiresome repetition of 'he or she', 'his or her' etc, masculine pronouns are used throughout this manual (unless the context otherwise requires) to denote persons who may be of either gender. We have made an exception for secretaries, who are assumed to be female for the reason that — at least at present — the vast majority of them are.

INTRODUCTION

This book is written for trainee solicitors, whether in large firms or small. Working in a solicitors' office can come as something of a shock. The transition from law school and the solicitors final examination to a solicitors' office can be daunting and frustrating. At college you were trained to consider legal issues within a narrowly defined syllabus. You will rapidly realise that in practice, client problems are not confined to just one area of the law, but may involve many issues, some of which you will not have studied. Moreover, the academic approach of most law degrees is very different from the requirements of a modern solicitor's practice.

When you first start your articles you may feel completely out of your depth. Do not be afraid, this is a common feeling. The majority of trainee solicitors suddenly realise that they have a great deal to learn about the practical application of the law.

Traditionally, an articled clerk would work closely with his principal, first merely observing and perhaps doing few relatively minor tasks. Gradually the articled clerk would be given a number of small jobs, still under close supervision. As the articled clerk became more familiar with legal practice a heavier workload and more responsible matters would be delegated to him.

Today, the pressure of a modern legal practice and increasing complexity of client work means that this relatively relaxed approach is increasingly unlikely. Today the trainee

1

solicitor is required to make a positive contribution to the firm in order to cover some of his overheads. Nevertheless, for most firms the cost of providing your training is expensive. In the case of some large city firms the cost inclusive of salaries, grants, training and other support may be as much as £75,000 per trainee.

In today's increasingly competitive environment the trainee solicitor must adopt a professional approach from the outset. Professionalism has little to do with a knowledge of the law itself; instead, it relates to the way you organise your work and your relationship to your clients, colleagues, staff, and other professionals. This book is designed to speed up the learning process, to guide you through the initial period of work in your office, to draw your awareness to a variety of professional skills.

First, some points to bear in mind right from the start:

(1) Do not be afraid to ask for help when you need it. Of course you want to make a good impression, and hence do not want to admit that you do not understand. But mistakes can be expensive, and can tarnish your firm's reputation. The standard required is high. If you got 80% in your exams, you probably got a first; if your work in the office is only 80% accurate, you risk a negligence action. We have all had to learn, and most of us remember how much support we needed. Of course senior staff are busy and working under pressure of time, but if you approach them at an appropriate moment they are usually willing to give the necessary guidance.

(2) Clients are entitled to expect that their affairs are being handled professionally and competently. Hence all your work must be accurate and of a high

standard. Be prepared to amend, revise and correct, rather than produce shoddy work. Your own reputation, and that of your firm, are immensely valuable. Once lost, they are difficult to recover.

(3) A lawyer's most valuable asset is his time. Hence you must be efficient and maximise the use of your time. If you do not organise yourself properly, your work will not reflect an effective use of time and you will produce exorbitant bills — for which no-one will thank you. Lawyers practise in a highly competitive world nowadays and must make sure that they give good value for money.

(4) Confidentiality is crucial. You must never discuss clients' affairs outside the office, however tempting it may be. The client must be able to have complete confidence that his private affairs will remain so. The most casual remark can cause embarrassment or financial loss. Even the fact that you are acting for a client at all is itself confidential, unless he chooses to make it common knowledge. If you should meet a client socially, for example, do not introduce him to others as your client but simply by name. Even when talking to other members of your firm, be careful what you say if there is the slightest possibility of outsiders overhearing it — e.g. from the waiting room.

(5) Solicitors are bound by undertakings, whether given personally or by another person within the firm. Hence as a trainee solicitor you should never give undertakings unless your principal specifically authorises you to do so.

(6) Never release any of the firm's papers or documents held on behalf of a client without the specific authority of a partner. The operation of a solicitor's

3

lien is a complex matter. It is explained in the Law Society's *Guide to Professional Practice*, and the Law Society will give telephone advice in times of pressing need.

Finally, the most important thing to remember is that you must always seek to learn from your experiences. Whenever you have completed a transaction, take the time to review your work. Ask yourself whether you could have done the task better and if so, how? Always record what you have done. Be wary of repeating the same learning curve time and time again. When you have completed the transaction set down all you have learnt. Then, each time you are involved in a similar transaction, revise your thoughts: is there any way you could have done the work better, how could you have done it faster, are there any points you need to tighten up on? By constantly seeking to refine your performance you will be enhancing and improving your skills. This will mean that your value as a solicitor will be increased.

SELF-PRESENTATION

This is a sensitive subject because most people regard their appearance as a matter personal to themselves — it is an expression of their personality, and they therefore object to having an image imposed upon them. To a degree this is true, but there is another side to the argument.

It may be unjust and irrational, but we all make fundamental judgments about each other within the first few minutes of meeting. Psychologists suggest that such judgments may be made in as little as two minutes. These judgments may change as we get to know one another better, but they may take some shifting. The usual image of a solicitor is of someone of smart, professional appearance, and people who cherish this notion may assume that if someone does not fit the image then he cannot be much of a lawyer. It is therefore advisable to conform to it unless and until you are sure that an alternative is acceptable in your firm. It is sensible to err on the side of formality rather than risk the reverse.

This is particularly true for a trainee solicitor. He is probably well aware of his lack of experience and how easily this may be revealed. If you look the part, you will have more credibility with clients, who will therefore be more willing to accept your advice. In addition, if you look the part you are more likely to have confidence in yourself.

Choose the clothes and grooming styles that are most helpful in creating the image you want. If such things as

reliability and security are involved, wear clothes that make little obvious impression but subliminally speak of power, confidence and success. Avoid bright colours, intricate patterns and outlandish styles. Your best bet is a dark well-cut suit. If your appearance indicates that you would rather be partying than doing business, getting serious attention from clients will an uphill struggle.

Of course, court attendances are a particular problem. If you are working in a litigation department it is sensible to dress in dark clothes all the time — you never know when you might be summoned to court with no warning. Even trainee solicitors have to attend before district judges, who are entitled to expect the respect due to a court; and, whether you like it or not, suitable dress is part of that respect. Anyway it will not do your self-confidence much good to have a district judge comment scathingly on your denims and orange T-shirt in front of your client and another solicitor.

THE LEGAL OFFICE

Every office has its own procedures, but some procedures are fundamental to the efficient running of any system. Indeed, they are so fundamental that other staff may assume that you know them without having to be told. This can be bewildering, and can lead to precious time being wasted in confusion.

The office day

You will probably have been told the office hours when you first started — they are likely to be something like 9.00 a.m. to 5.30 p.m. You will soon find out that they are of little relevance to you beyond indicating when the office staff will be available. Eyebrows will soon be raised if you regard these hours as a rigid demarcation of your responsibilities. All professionals have to work odd hours on occasion, sometimes at short notice. If you are given a task to complete by a specified deadline, you must do so even if it does involve working late. Law is now a competitive profession, and solicitors have to be available when the client needs them — even if it is at two in the morning. Obviously you are entitled to have commitments outside the office, but be sensible about them.

The office day is usually structured around various important times. In particular, you should know:

(a) when the post leaves the office;
(b) when letters are taken to the Document Exchange (DX) system; and
(c) who has authority to sign cheques, invoices and possibly letters — and when that person leaves the office.

Of course, documents can be sent outside normal office hours by fax. However, this does not always help if there is no-one at the other end to receive your message!

Office staff

Secretarial and administrative support will vary enormously from firm to firm, and you must find out who you should ask to do work for you. Always give a secretary clear instructions and allow enough time for the work to be done. Remember that she will undoubtedly have work to do for other people and that yours is unlikely to be given a high priority. When it comes back to you it is your responsibility to check it very carefully. This is not the secretary's job. Remember that it gives a bad impression of the firm if letters are misspelt, confused or ungrammatical.

You should also make a habit of notifying the secretary who does your work (or the switchboard operator, depending on the procedure in your firm) of your whereabouts. It is not fair on her if she is left dealing with angry clients who want to contact you and she does not know where you are. It is also a poor reflection on you and on the firm.

Do not make the mistake of trying to boost your own morale by talking down to the office staff. You may have passed your exams, but they are probably far more experienced than you and can teach you a lot. And *never* take your feelings out on them. Treat them as specialists in what

they do. You need their support and will be much more productive if you are regarded by your secretary as a good person to work with.

Many lawyers fail to use their secretaries effectively. Very often the approach adopted is not to say precisely what is wanted but to criticise the secretary when she gets it wrong. Such lawyers would find that spending more time working with their secretary, exchanging information and ideas and developing a professional relationship, would be much more productive. Particularly when you first join the firm your secretary is likely to know much more about the firm's procedures and have more experience of working in a solicitors' office than you do. When you are told who will be doing your work you should take an opportunity to discuss how things are or could be done, and see if your new secretary has any ideas or preferences of her own.

It is likely that when you first join the firm you will not have your own secretary. You may be required to share with other trainees, or possibly use your principal's secretary. In that case the more experienced solicitor may wish to pull rank to ensure that their work is completed first. In the first instance you may discuss scheduling of work with the secretary. However, if she is not able to accommodate your work on time do not take this personally. It may be that she is simply doing as she is told. In that case it would be preferable to discuss getting your work done with whoever else shares the secretary.

The filing system

Find out as soon as possible how your particular system works. You will be lost until you master this, because the files are the record of all work done for clients. The essential purposes of a filing system are the storage and retrieval of

information. Every letter written, every document drafted and every form filled in on behalf of a client must be kept on the relevant file, so that in the future anyone can see quickly what has been done.

Precisely because files must serve as an efficient method of finding out what has been done, it is important that you comply with your firm's indexing or numbering system. There is nothing more frustrating than wasting time trying to find documents which have been incorrectly filed. If they are deeds this can be disastrous! Another way to avoid misfiling is to make sure that a file reference is included on all correspondence.

Files must be kept for at least six years, and many firms keep them for much longer. For many purposes six years is the basic limitation period, but remember that in some cases the limitation period is longer. The Latent Damage Act 1986, for example, provides for a 'long-stop' of fifteen years.

Your firm will have a system which must be followed when creating a new file. There may also be standard instructions relating to recording key information. If there is no specific practice adopted by your firm it may be helpful if you inscribe somewhere obvious (e.g. on the inside of the cover) the phone and fax numbers of the client, other firms involved, counsel etc.

Some bewilderment may be avoided if you bear in mind that it is not practicable to insert new material at the back of the file, because you would have to remove all the existing contents first. So you insert the new material at the front. This means that the file reads from back to front. It also means that documents usually appear in the order in which they were inserted, not necessarily that in which they were created. A fax, for example, is often confirmed by a hard copy which is sent by post or document exchange. If they are both filed upon receipt they may be some distance apart in the file. You may find it helpful to tag certain pages of a file with 'stickies', to save having to thumb right through the file every time you want to refer to (e.g.) a crucial letter.

For further details, see the chapter on file management.

OFFICE EQUIPMENT

The technology available in the average office has changed enormously in the past few years, and will undoubtedly continue to do so. However, the following are now fairly standard.

Photocopier

Modern practice does, of course, rely heavily on photocopiers. But remember that you may not have to copy the document bundle yourself. Even with the machines now available, photocopying can take a very long time. So delegate whenever possible — there may, for example, be someone employed for just this purpose. And allow adequate time for the work to be done.

Whoever does the copying, a careful file note should be kept of the number of copies made, since this may be relevant to your client's bill.

Fax machine

Fax (short for facsimile exchange) has revolutionised office practice. It enables a document to be copied from one machine to another, perhaps on the other side of the world. It does this by converting the physical image of the document into a digital signal, which is then transmitted down a telephone line and reconstructed by the machine at the other

15

end. Written messages or copy documents may be transferred within minutes or (if they are short) seconds. Hence many legal processes have been speeded up enormously. Fax may be used (e.g.) to send an urgent brief to counsel, or to agree last-minute amendments to documents. Sometimes even routine letters are faxed, the 'hard' (i.e. typed) copy following on behind. The machine normally has its own telephone line and automatically receives any documents sent to it. Hence messages can be sent outside normal office hours and after the last post has gone.

The advantages are obvious. No longer do you have to wait until a hard-pressed secretary has time to type your letters, hopefully in time to catch the post. In the interests of speed, hand-written messages may occasionally be acceptable. Just be careful to check you have authority for what you write — it is just as binding! The disadvantage of the speed and informality is that many offices are geared round the delivery of the post, and there may not be an adequate system for collecting fax messages. So, ironically, a message which is sent by fax because it is urgent may sit in the recipient machine for a couple of hours before anyone notices it. Hence it may be sensible to ring to warn of arrival.

It is important to remember that fax machines may be located in a general office or a relatively public place. If you are sending confidential information it is imperative that you phone the recipient so that they can be ready to collect the fax as it comes off the machine.

The system is relatively fool-proof and cheap. All you have to do to send a message is to put the document in position, dial the number of the recipient machine and press the start button. Your piece of paper will be sucked through and a copy of it sent to the other party, leaving you with your own copy. As your document enters the machine, a copy is emerging from the machine at the other end of the line. You do not even have to wait until the machine has finished, since it will stop automatically and will warn you if a page has not gone through properly. But if you are sending more than one sheet you may need to start feeding each one in as the last one disappears: otherwise the machine may assume that you have finished, and switch itself off. If you started (as you should) with a cover sheet saying who the fax is coming from and how many pages there are, the recipient will instantly be on the phone demanding to know where the rest of it is.

The machine even keeps a record of all calls made and the length of time they took, which, if put on file, is invaluable when you later come to bill the client.

The main thing to check when sending a fax is that you are sending the message to the right person. It is not a good idea to send a message intended for the client, or counsel, to the other side! Make sure, also, that you dial the recipient's fax number — not his phone number.

The quality of paper used in most fax machines is not at the moment as good as that used by photocopiers. Nor do they generally produce such good print. It is particularly important to remember that fax machines use heat-sensitive paper, so that in time the print disappears. If fax messages are left in sunlight they will be illegible in a matter of days. Hence important messages or documents should always be photocopied — you will look a little silly if all you can produce in court is a blank piece of paper!

There is also a minor risk that the machine may damage the document as it sends the copy. Hence important documents should also be photocopied before sending. (Documents on thick paper may not be accepted by the machine anyway.) Also remove any staples or paper clips which might damage the machine.

Word processors

The increased use of word-processors has also made a major change to legal practice. If a document, e.g. a will, has to be amended to reflect the client's instructions, a secretary no longer has to laboriously type the whole thing out again. Similarly a lease can be easily adapted as the parties negotiate terms. This means that it is much easier to amend documents, particularly lengthy documents. Remember to use this facility. You must thoroughly revise, check and double check your letters and documents.

Many firms now have large precedent banks and standard-form letters for common transactions. These save an enormous amount of time on routine matters, but they have their own dangers. The risk is that when we are in a hurry we tend to add on to them what we need, without deleting what we do not need. Leases, for example, are getting bigger and bigger by the day. Whilst size is not necessarily a problem, it would be unfortunate if the agreement contained inconsistent or contradictory clauses.

Where precedents have been amended, give clear instructions to the WP operator. All documents must be carefully checked to ensure that they meet the client's needs. If a document has been amended a number of times you should carefully check to ensure that you receive the latest draft. Do not assume that previous amendments are always incorporated. The WP operator ought to keep on disk a copy (and a back-up copy) of everything she types, unless told otherwise. But to err is human. Keep a hard copy of anything you cannot live without!

Some of the secretaries may have machines which fall somewhere between a conventional typewriter and a fully-fledged WP: it may be possible to correct minor errors without retyping the whole document, but not to make wholesale changes to the document's structure. Find out what can be done and make the most of the technology available, but don't ask the impossible.

FILE MANAGEMENT

At first you may deal with a couple of files of your own, under the close supervision of your principal. Eventually, when you qualify, you may have hundreds. To manage this number requires organisation — your files must be systematically and effectively managed. The file should be sufficiently comprehensive so that someone looking at the file can understand exactly what has taken place.

You may be actually handling a particular matter, but the file remains the property of the firm. Others must be able to read the file and see from it precisely what has been done on that matter. You may be ill or go on holiday, and others will have to carry on your work. You must not rely on your memory, because as you deal with a greater volume of work you will simply not be able to remember in sufficient detail what you did on each file. So everything you do must be meticulously noted on the file in date order, and tied down, as a record of the life of that transaction.

Attendance notes

It is essential that you make a full attendance note for the file whenever you speak to anyone — whether the client, counsel, another firm or anyone else, and whether in person or on the phone. If you make a visit elsewhere on behalf of the client, e.g. attending at court, a full note must be made. This should be done as soon as possible, while your recollection is clear, so that the note is as accurate and complete as possible. It should indicate who you are, the time, date and place of the discussion, and how long it took. And it is essential to note any instructions from the client, anything you have said you will do, and any advice given. Of course the attendance note is not only a record of what has happened, but also an aid in time costing. It is particularly important because a time costing sheet will not usually be accepted on taxation unless supported by a full attendance note.

WHAT TO INCLUDE IN AN ATTENDANCE NOTE

(1) Date, time and length of the meeting.
(2) Persons in attendance.
(3) Documents distributed.
(4) Information given by both sides.
(5) Advice.
(6) Client's instructions, if any.
(7) Decisions or agreements reached.
(8) Action, who is to do what, deadline.

Opening new files

In order that your file can be an efficient record of the life of the transaction it is sensible to open a separate file for each matter, even if they are related. For example, in a conveyancing matter, combining a sale and purchase in one file inevitably leads to confusion. Also, check that no-one else has already opened a file, so that yours only receives half the necessary papers!

Many firms' file references use a combination of client and transaction numbers. This means that a client will have the same client number however many matters the firm handles for that client. If you are handling a number of transactions for a client you must ensure that correspondence is entered onto the correct file. If you think it may be helpful, put copies of correspondence, documents, notes etc onto other files. In that case, clearly indicate it is a copy.

Keep the file strictly in date order, working from back to front, so that you can readily find the information you need. Also ensure copies of all correspondence and other documentation are kept — if you file a form at the Companies Registry, for example, retain a copy of it for future reference.

Reminder system

Keep your files under constant review. Missed deadlines and time limits are a major cause of negligence actions, which can be avoided by checking carefully that you act as and when needed. Use check-lists where possible to help you. These are lists of what needs doing in standard transactions, and may be pinned to the front of the file. In this way you reduce the risk of missing deadlines or of turning up to a completion without the building society cheque!

All future commitments should be incorporated into a reminder system. This will include all dates relating to court matters including limitation dates, deadline dates for various pleadings, deadlines for notice of appeal, disposition dates and trial and hearing dates. Moreover in non-contentious matters check carefully what deadlines are appropriate, for example follow up dates for lease renewals, rent reviews, share options, or Company House filing requirements.

In addition to the above you should regularly ensure that your client is briefed on the progress of the matter. Many clients express dissatisfaction with the delay experienced in legal work and the lack of information they receive. You should schedule a regular review of all your files, and use that as an opportunity for client care. You may perhaps phone or write to your client to indicate what has taken place and what you are currently doing. Schedule this at a time which is convenient to yourself. You will undoubtedly find that your clients will be appreciative of this service.

Many firms will have developed a firm-wide reminder system. If your firm has, you must make sure that you are thoroughly familiar with the system and adopt it. If the firm has not developed such a system you should establish your own, possibly in conjunction with your secretary. You may perhaps wish to develop a standard form which should include at least the following information:

(1) Client's name and the file number.
(2) A description of the transaction and, if appropriate, court references etc.
(3) A description of the action you are to take.
(4) The deadline date.
(5) The date on which you should work on the matter in order not to miss the deadline. You may wish to give yourself at least one working week in order to complete the work, get it typed and reviewed.
(6) Reminder perhaps two or three days before the action date.

If you have a secretary who is responsible for all your work she may be asked to manage the reminder system, ensuring that each reminder and file is brought to you.

'Hand-me-down' files

The trainee solicitor tends to get the 'hand-me-down' files on which essentials may be missing, or where the matter has been left for some time. So read the file fully and carefully before you act, or you may end up doing work which is unnecessary or contrary to your instructions. Carefully check that your client's requirements have been ascertained and fulfilled and all correspondence answered. If there are any problems, ask the person who dealt with the matter before. Also check whether there are any relevant time limits — the three-month limit on an unfair dismissal claim, for example, disappears very fast. Remember that you may have been given the file precisely because there is a problem in it. If there is anything wrong, tell someone quickly. If a mistake is discovered in time it may be possible to remedy it, but the longer it is left the harder this becomes.

CHARGING

While you are struggling to cope with the everyday crises of office life, it is easy to forget one of the main reasons for your being there in the first place: viz. to help the business make enough profit to enable the partners and staff to earn their living. You will not, of course, be directly involved in the business decisions of the practice just yet; but it helps to have a basic understanding of the financial considerations involved.

The firm's profitability (or otherwise) depends on both its income and its expenditure — which are in turn related to the amount of work being done. But the relationship between work and income is much closer than that between work and expenditure. This is because the expenditure includes not only 'variable costs', which increase according to the volume of work being done (e.g. phone bills, postage and stationery), but also 'fixed costs', which do not (e.g. rent, salaries and depreciation); and the fixed costs in a solicitors' practice tend to be much bigger than the variable ones. This means that most of the firm's expenditure has to be incurred regardless of whether much income is earned. It follows that the firm has to obtain a certain amount of work (and therefore earn income) simply to cover its costs, i.e. in order to 'break even'. Once this point has been passed, there are no further costs apart from the (comparatively small) variable costs associated with further activity. Most of the income derived from any additional work beyond this break-even point will therefore be profit, available for drawing by the partners and/or ploughing back into the business.

These considerations become directly relevant when you have to decide how much to charge for a particular job. It goes without saying that you must make a careful note of all the time spent on a matter — e.g. attending the client, telephone calls, preparing documents, attending court etc. Solicitors are in the business of 'selling time', and you cannot charge a client for your time unless you know how much of it he has had.

But you need to know other things too. For a start, you must know how much your time actually *costs*: otherwise you may end up selling it at a loss, which will not endear you to the partners. The 'expense of time' is calculated according to a complicated formula laid down by the Law Society. This involves taking the firm's estimated expenditure over a period of time, and adding a notional figure for partners' salaries (at assistant solicitor rates!). This gives a projected total expense. A small part of this is assumed to be recoverable from retained interest on client monies, but the rest has to be recovered by doing chargeable work. Each fee earner is charged with his own salary (real or notional) and with an appropriate proportion of the firm's other expenditure; this gives the total expenditure associated with each individual. This figure is then spread across the chargeable hours which that individual is expected to work, thus giving an hourly expense rate. This rate, when applied to the time recorded against a particular matter and compared with the actual charge to the client, will show how much profit (or loss) that matter produced.

But the hourly expense rate is not an infallible guide to the appropriate charge. The time recorded may be excessive for the job, or the cost of that time may be unduly high in relation to the value of the work done — or, of course, unduly low. Also bear in mind that if the charging rates used are no higher than those emerging from the expense of time calculation, and the expected chargeable time is worked, the amount left over (after expenditure) will be sufficient only to pay the partners their notional salaries — with no reward for the additional skill and responsibility of a partner, or for the risks involved in being in business. In addition nothing will be left to plough back into the business to safeguard its future.

Moreover, solicitors' charges are governed by legislation as well as by contract. Under these rules, no less than seven factors are to be taken into account:

(1) the complexity, difficulty or novelty of the matter;
(2) the skill, labour, specialised knowledge and responsibility involved;
(3) the time spent on the matter;
(4) the number and importance of the documents prepared or perused;
(5) the place where the business is transacted;
(6) the amount or value of money or property involved (and, in the case of the Probate Costs Rules, its nature); and
(7) the importance of the matter to the client.

In other words, the time expended is only one factor among many. This is because the hourly charging rate represents only the *cost* of the time expended: in arriving at the amount to be actually charged, that cost will have 'value' added to it. This is done by applying a 'mark-up', which varies enormously between different types of work (and even different parts of the country), and/or a 'value factor' which reflects the values involved in the transaction. It is therefore vital to record not only *how much* time is spent on each matter, but also *how* that time is spent.

27

What this boils down to is that you must make sure you are not charging less than the work justifies. But make sure you are not charging more, either! Remember that the client has two alternative remedies if he feels he has been overcharged. First, he can apply to the court for an order that the bill be taxed (i.e. vetted and certified) by the court under the Solicitors Act 1974.

This is something of risk, since the costs of the taxation will be added to the bill unless at least one-fifth of the bill is taxed off (in which case the costs will be borne by the solicitor). The alternative, which costs the client nothing, is to ask the solicitor to obtain a remuneration certificate under the Solicitors' Remuneration Order 1972. This is a certificate issued by the Law Society, after inspecting the solicitor's file and considering his explanation of his charges, stating either that in the Society's opinion the sum charged is fair and reasonable, or what sum *would* be fair and reasonable. Obviously the client need only pay the amount thus certified. But if he wants a certificate he must ask for it within one month of being told of his right to one. (There is no such right in the case of bills for contentious business: the appropriate remedy is to get the bill taxed by the court.)

One last complication: many firms now operate a time-recording system which uses an 'achieve rate' rather than a rate reflecting the expense of time. This means that individuals are charged out at standard rates which include:

(a) the cost of the individual;
(b) the overheads associated with the individual; and
(c) a profit element,

and which reflect the individual's skill and experience and the type of work he generally undertakes. Such a rate thus represents not only an hourly expense rate, but mark-up and value added as well. Find out which system you are supposed to use!

Time sheets

Virtually every firm these days will require you to keep time sheets. The time sheets will require you indicate in six-minute or possibly ten-minute units what you have done during the day.

At first this may seem to be particularly onerous, but once you have developed a system it should not cause you too much difficulty. The secret with time sheets is to record information regularly. If you try to complete the time sheet at the end of the day, or worse still at the end of the week, you will find it difficult. However, if you prepare the time sheet as you are doing your work, possibly on an hourly basis, it should present no great difficulty.

Many junior solicitors, particularly those who are given fee targets to achieve, feel that the time recording system is a tremendous advantage to them. It doesn't matter how efficiently they work — provided they put their time to a client, they are achieving their targets. This attitude is very short-sighted. Obviously your clients will take into account how efficiently you work and the size of their ultimate bill. Always bear in mind the need to work efficiently so that you are doing a job in a reasonable time scale.

There will be various grey areas where you will need to liaise with the firm to determine its approach. These grey areas include:

(1) To what extent should the client pay for your learning curve? If you are given a new task and spend a disproportionate amount of time on that matter because it is new to you, to what extent

should the client be charged for all your time?

(2) If you are working with another more senior lawyer — attending meetings, reviewing the file etc — to what extent should your time be charged to the client in addition to the other lawyers?

(3) You will be asked to research points of law on behalf of a client: how much of that research can be charged to the client, and what happens if the research is subsequently used for other clients' work?

(4) Very often a lawyer who is handling a transaction would like to bounce ideas off other lawyers in the firm, particularly if the other lawyer is a specialist in (for example) tax, employment etc. In those circumstances, to what extent should the client be charged for both lawyers' time?

You should carefully record how you spend your time. Ascertain your firm's policy with regards to the above and other grey areas. If appropriate, make a note on the file to indicate what you have done and draw this matter to the attention of the partner or fee earner preparing the bill.

TIME MANAGEMENT

Time is your most precious professional commodity. By using it effectively you can achieve more in terms of chargeable output. A little thought can make an enormous difference to what you achieve in a day. We all have the same amount of time in any given day, and cannot save it up — if you do not use your time effectively today, it is lost for good.

Of course everybody works differently; but there are general guidelines which are applicable to all. They will help you use your time more efficiently, and will provide a basis for your personal work patterns.

You have four choices in dealing with a given piece of work. You can:

(a) not do it at all;
(b) postpone it;
(c) delegate it; or
(d) do it yourself.

Not doing a piece of work at all

The temptation is to take on everything that comes your way in order to impress your principal. This is dangerous even when you are qualified, and all the more so while you are still learning. If you have too much work on, or you take on work which you are not qualified to do, you will make mistakes. Many negligence actions against solicitors are simply the

32

result of overwork. Only take on work which you can do effectively. If necessary discuss your workload with your principal.

If you are being given work by a number of people in your practice the danger you will face is that no-one fully appreciates how much you have to undertake. In this situation it is important that you carefully assess your overall workload and when you will be able to complete a given task. Whenever you are given work always ask what the deadline is. If you have incompatible deadlines it is preferable to raise the issue then. Do not take work on if you are unable to complete it by the specified deadline. The fee earner who gave the task to you will be relying on you.

Postponing work

This is a positive method of controlling your work, not a way of avoiding it. One matter may not be as urgent as another, so you may make a conscious decision to delay doing anything about it until a more appropriate time in the future. But this requires organisation on your part. You must stay in control. You must watch the file in case it becomes urgent. You must allocate a time when it *is* appropriate to act, and not forget about it. This enables you to plan the use of your time in advance.

As indicated above whenever you are given a project, you must always ascertain the deadline. Do not assume that work can wait. It is up to you to check when work is required. Only then can you seek to schedule your work.

Delegation

Of course, as a trainee solicitor you will be the humble recipient of much work delegated by others. They are simply

35

trying to use their own time efficiently by giving you the more straightforward work from which you can safely learn. But remember that you *are* learning, and are therefore entitled to insist on clear instructions and to ask questions when in doubt. Never take risks, because no-one will thank you when you made a mistake which has to be (or cannot be) rectified.

In addition, you in your turn may be able to delegate some of your routine matters. It is all a question of cost-effectiveness and time-efficiency. If there is an office junior and your time could be more profitably spent, delegate the photocopying and other mundane duties. But remember to give clear instructions, and allow the junior to ask you questions if necessary.

Doing work yourself

Throughout your legal career you will generally find that you will have to cope with a large volume of work, often subject to tight deadlines. If you are to be on top of your workload you must ensure that you are properly organised. Planning and organisation is the key to maximising your efficiency and work output. Without planning and organisation you have no means of ensuring that your work is completed on time and to an appropriate standard.

The next section will consider various techniques to enable you to organise your work flow.

Personal organisation

THE DIARY

One of the essentials of good time management is effective use of your diary. Your diary should be used for three purposes:-

    (a) to record notices, deadlines, time limits;
    (b) to schedule appointments;
    (c) to plan your work.

NOTICES

We have already noted in the section on file management that you should devise a system of reminders to ensure that you do not miss deadlines, time limits or other important time constraints. You should also use your diary for this purpose as a form of double check. Always remember that you should not only include time limits and deadlines but should also give yourself sufficient advanced warning to enable the task to be completed on time.

APPOINTMENTS

Most people use their diary to record the start of appointments (for example, clients, witnesses, other solicitors). As you enter these appointments you should block out enough time to enable you to deal with them. It is rude to rush off from a meeting, or to keep others waiting for you. It suggests lack of organisation on your part and an assumption that your time is more important than that of other people. In addition, by scheduling the estimated ending of a meeting you are better able to assess how much free time you have during the day for other matters.

Not only should you schedule the estimated ending time for the meeting, you should also try to ensure that the meeting actually does conclude at that time. To enable you to do this, when arranging meetings you should give an indication of how long you estimate the meeting will take. This will be particularly well received by clients, who are frequently unsure how long they should allow for a meeting with their solicitor. If someone asks you to attend a meeting you should courteously ask how long they estimate the meeting will take.

Then when the meeting starts you may refer to the estimated duration of the meeting to get the parties focusing on how long the meeting should take.

Prior to the meeting you should always allocate time to enable you to prepare properly. You will do yourself, your firm or client no good by arriving ill-prepared at meetings.

You should also schedule time after the meeting to deal with any correspondence that has arisen and to prepare your attendance note. It is advisable to schedule this time immediately after your meeting. This has the advantage that if the meeting runs over, you will have time available. Moreover you will find that the detail of the meeting is fresh in your memory. You are more likely to interpret your hand-written notes and will take you far less time to deal with the correspondence. If you leave the follow-up correspondence until later in the day, or possibly into the next day, you will find it much harder to recall what was discussed, to decipher your attendance note and to complete the necessary documentation.

PLANNING YOUR WORK

In addition to your diary you should maintain a 'things to do' list. If you have a large number of transactions to undertake there is the risk that you will overlook something. Systematically recording and listing all the jobs that you have to do will give you a far greater sense of control.

Once you have created your first 'things to do' list you should ensure that it is regularly maintained. Every time you are given a new assignment, add it to the list. Regularly arrange for your secretary to retype the list. Particularly if your office has word processing facilities, this should not be a major task. This means that you will have a constant record of all the jobs you must undertake.

The preparation of a 'things to do' list may, in itself, reduce the pressure on you; nevertheless it can be fairly daunting to see a lengthy list. You should therefore estimate how long you feel each task should take. Do this in hourly units. At first you will probably find that you are greatly underestimating how long each task will take. However, with experience you will find that you can much more accurately predict how long a job will last. Having done that, you should then decide when you plan to do your work. It is unlikely that you will be able to complete all your tasks within one day. You must therefore prioritise to determine which tasks you wish to complete first and when you have time to do them.

To enable you to anticipate and properly schedule your workload, you should allow approximately half an hour each week to carefully review the next four to five weeks. This will give you the opportunity to think ahead, to calculate what you have to do and decide when you are to do it.

Once you have determined your priorities and decided when you wish to do your work, enter that into your diary. It is advisable that you do this in pencil as your priorities are likely to change.

If you have a number of large projects which will take many hours to complete, you may find that it is difficult to devote yourself to those tasks to the exclusion of other work. It is advisable in that case to try to break down the large projects into a number of smaller tasks. Those tasks can then more easily be scheduled into your diary. The process of breaking down large tasks into smaller units also has the advantage of giving you a number of review dates to ensure that the project is proceeding on schedule. Moreover, you will feel much more enthusiastic and in control of your work as you see the various sections being done.

THE DAILY PLAN

In addition to the meticulous use of your diary, and your 'things to do' list, you should also prepare a daily plan each evening before you go home from work to identify precisely what you intend to do the next day.

It has been said that the preparation of a daily plan is one of the most effective ways of controlling your time and ensuring you get the maximum amount of work done in any day.

The advantages of preparing a daily plan are as follows:

(1) You can review your diary, 'things to do' list, and activities during the day to correctly determine your priorities for tomorrow.

(2) When you arrive at the office the next day, rather than sorting through the papers on your desk, you will know exactly what you should start work on.

(3) By preparing the daily plan the night before, you are less likely to procrastinate and put off unpleasant or difficult tasks. If you try to prepare your daily schedule in the morning, at the start of the day you are more likely to defer difficult or unpleasant tasks.

(4) You have a feeling of control knowing exactly what you have to do the next day. This hopefully will give you a relaxed evening.

When you are organising your day and preparing your daily plan, try to adopt the strategy of never putting low priority work before high priority work. Many people when they first arrive at their offices tend to concentrate on miscellaneous low priority tasks in order to clear their desks for more important work later. The danger of this is that the low priority tasks generally take longer than anticipated, moreover, they will be interrupted and other priorities and tasks will emerge. The effect of this is that the more important jobs that are left will not be done. It is far more sensible to concentrate on the most important task first, and only when that is finished move to less urgent and less important tasks.

Common problem areas, and how to avoid them

In this section we focus on problems which are commonly encountered by trainee solicitors and other lawyers in practice. When you first join the firm it is easy to feel that you are the only person who is having difficulty managing your workload and being efficient. When you have been in the firm a little longer you will appreciate that many (if not all) the fee earners will experience the same anxiety and will be striving for greater efficiency.

Listed below are various factors which professionals generally find adversely affect their efficient time management:

INTERRUPTIONS

Probably the most frequent complaint of solicitors is the number of interruptions to their work. A busy solicitor may be subject to sixty to eighty interruptions per day. When you bear in mind that sixty interruptions per day is an interruption every eight minutes, it makes you realise just how much time is taken by interruptions.

When you first start your articles it is difficult to prevent interruptions. Other members of your firm would not

41

be impressed if, for example, you tried to divert calls or tried to implement a closed door policy. When you become more senior you may wish to schedule periods during the day when you will not receive interruptions and during which you will concentrate on important work.

In the meantime, the best way to avoid interruptions is to try to anticipate the requirements of your clients and other members of your firm. For example, many solicitors will be driven to distraction by clients phoning to check routine matters at a time when they are very busy. This sort of problem could easily be overcome if the solicitor were to take the initiative and contact clients at a time convenient to him. You may possibly consider scheduling a regular review, possibly aiming to review each file every three weeks, to contact your clients to let them know what the current position is. In certain circumstances it may be appropriate that this is contact is made by letter, briefly explaining the position and indicating what you are doing.

ATTEMPTING TOO MUCH

A new trainee solicitor will be anxious to impress and will generally be very willing to help other members of the firm. However, if you take on too much your efficiency will dramatically decline and your ability to give detailed attention to your work will be reduced. This can be a particular problem for the trainee solicitor who receives work from a variety of sources. At the end of the day it is up to you to maintain control over your workload to ensure that you are not taking on too much. Obviously you should not say 'no' to a task, but it is perfectly acceptable for you to discuss your work commitments with your principal and ask for relief from certain projects or at least a longer time scale to complete them in.

PERSONAL DISORGANISATION — CLUTTERED DESK

As a new trainee solicitor you may find that you are required to fit into someone else's office. You may not have a great deal of personal working space and in some cases may not even have your own desk.

If the accommodation and space available to you is limited it is essential that you organise it efficiently.

If you fail to organise your correspondence properly you will spend a great deal of time sorting through your papers trying to find documents, letters etc. You should try to ensure from the outset that you adopt a systematic and thorough personal filing system. Ideally you should use your desk as a tool to process work, not as a place to store work. If you have sufficient space, you should aim to keep current files and other matters you wish to keep close on a separate table so as to leave your desk free for the task you are now working on. If the space is very limited, and you have to use your desk for your current files, it is essential that you maintain an orderly system. A great deal of time can be wasted if papers are put into the wrong file. It has been said that you can tell a well-organised person by the state of his desk. Do not be guided on this matter by other colleagues in your office. Be ruthless in keeping your working space well organised and tidy. Aim to file correspondence as soon as possible and return it to the filing system. Only if it is absolutely essential to retain files should you keep them.

LACK OF SELF-DISCIPLINE — PROCRASTINATION

Self-discipline is fundamental to sound management and therefore to sound time management. Always remember that it is up to you to manage your own time. Be assertive, take

44

control of your time, carefully plan what you intend to do during the day. To help you do this, prepare your daily plan the night before. Once you have done that, it is essential that you commit yourself to working to that daily plan. Avoid the temptation to put off work, to day-dream and to socialise. Remember that your firm will judge you by the efficiency with which you deal with your work. Avoid putting off difficult or unpleasant tasks. Get into the habit of dealing with only one task at a time. Once you have started it, aim to complete it. Be ruthless with yourself, force through your work, perhaps planning a treat or a break once you have completed the task.

SOCIALISING

Of course there must always be room for a little socialising at work; it establishes good relations and adds zest to life. However, socialising is a major time waster — it can be particularly problematic when you are busy and other people fail to recognise that.

Make sure that you do not unnecessarily disturb other people by your socialising. Remember there must be a balance and it is better if you complete your work.

If you find you are being interrupted by other people wishing to socialise, try to adopt the strategy of getting up and walking to them when they enter your room. Try to give no opportunity to the person to settle down for a long discussion. In a severe case it may appropriate to explain to other people that you have an urgent project to complete and you need to concentrate on your work. Whilst it can be difficult to put people off, if handled tactfully other people can get the message without being affronted.

TELEPHONES

The modern solicitor spends more and more of his time on the telephone, because it is so much quicker and more convenient than travelling to see people face to face. Yet a surprising number of people are wary of using the phone. Even those who are confident often do not perform as they would if the person they are speaking to were in front of them. (It is interesting that even experienced negotiators often perform noticeably less well on the phone than in person.)

When we talk to another person face-to-face the words we use are only one method of communication. We receive messages from the other person's expressions, gestures and posture. None of this is possible on the phone, and a whole range of communication has been lost. Hence it is more difficult to establish rapport and it is easier to jump to the wrong conclusions. One of you may lose concentration, simply because most people find it easier to remember what they see than what they hear. It is significant that most people find it easier to talk to someone on the phone if they have met them, because they can then visualise them.

Provided that you carefully identify what you are trying to achieve, a considerable amount of time can be saved by discussing matters over the phone rather than arranging a meeting. Even if a meeting is held close to your office it will generally take far longer than a telephone conversation, and if travel expenses are incurred it can prove far more expensive. When you are thinking of arranging a meeting, always ask yourself if it is necessary to do so and whether you could satisfactorily achieve your purpose over the phone. However, remember the following advantages of a face to face meeting:

(1) Meetings are better for establishing personal relationships. It is easier to build up a rapport with someone you meet rather than someone you talk to over the phone. For this purpose it is advisable to arrange to meet, particularly at the start of a transaction.

(2) Whilst it is possible to assess the other party's reaction over the phone, you can generally get a much better insight to their reactions when you meet face to face.

(3) It is possible to discuss detailed documentation over the phone, but it is far easier to do so in a meeting where you can more easily focus on the issues.

(4) Where a number of people are likely to be involved, a meeting is preferable. It is possible to conduct a meeting with a number of people by using a conference phone. However, it is generally not that easy to set up such a facility.

In the legal office it is the person who makes the call who is initially in control, because he is doing so when it is convenient for him and when he is prepared for it. Before you make a call you should have the relevant file in front of you, and have decided what you want to achieve and what you will say in order to achieve it. This way you are less likely to be flustered and thrown by the other party. You will be more relaxed if you are organised, so that you can think straight — as soon as you become tense, your brain will cease to work properly.

Always introduce yourself, adding the name of your

firm, and ascertain who you are speaking to. Remember that your duty of confidentiality demands that you do not disclose information unless you are speaking to the right person. Explain why you are ringing and speak clearly at a reasonable speed. Always make notes during the conversation: if you rely on your memory, for even the simplest query, you will find that ten minutes later you are not quite sure whether the other person said 'yes' or 'no'. While you are making notes of what the other person says, let him know that you are still listening by making the occasional encouraging noise. Conclude the conversation by summarising what has been said and telling the other party what is to be done as a result.

Remember that clients may be nervous of talking to a solicitor (especially on the phone!) and therefore may not listen accurately. So give them a chance to ask questions, and ask whether everything is clear. Even then it is necessary to confirm in writing any conclusion or advice, partly because memory plays tricks and partly because a letter makes the client feel looked after. Always make an attendance note and any necessary diary entries as soon as possible.

You are in a more vulnerable position if you are the recipient of the call, since you may be buried in another matter, and you probably will not have the file in front of you. If it is not possible for you to take the call, explain why and promise to ring back — then do so! If you are willing to take the call, you are entitled to ask the caller to hold for a minute while you get the file. You should never try to bluff your way through or let a solicitor harass you into giving information when you are not sure of your ground. The danger is that, because the caller does not know you are a trainee, you may try to bluff and appear to know more than perhaps you do. That way expensive mistakes are made. Keep in control. If you do not know, say so, and volunteer to find out and ring back. Always be careful what you say.

Remember that a contract or an undertaking can be entered into on the phone. When dealing with the other side in litigation, make sure that it is clear from the outset whether or not the conversation is without prejudice.

Very often when you are trying to speak to someone on the phone your plans are put out because of the following:

(a) the person you are ringing is not available;
(b) you have left a message asking to be rung back but your call is not returned;
(c) the person you are ringing is engaged on the telephone and the receptionist put you on hold.

The best approach to deal with this, if the person you wish to speak to is not available, is to ask to speak to his or her secretary. Arrange with the secretary when it will be convenient for you to return the call. Indicate to the secretary what you wish to talk about and ask that she arranges to have the relevant papers available. This will ensure that you have a relatively good prospect of making contact at a time that is convenient for you. Moreover, when you make your call the person you wish to speak to will be properly briefed and prepared.

As a trainee solicitor you will be frequently asked to take calls for your principal at a time when your principal is not available. When taking the call you should:

(a) obtain the name of the caller and where appropriate, details of the firm/company and telephone number;
(b) ascertain the purpose of the call;
(c) ascertain when the caller would be available for your principal to return the call;
(d) prepare a message for your principal;
(e) give the message and the relevant file to your

principal for his attention.

Finally, the most important point to appreciate is that whenever you take a telephone call you represent the firm. Always be courteous even if you are not the person who should be taking the call. The person you are speaking to does not know your position; as far as they are concerned *you* are the firm.

DICTATION

The dictaphone is a blessing in the modern office, because it is so quick (about seven times faster than writing longhand). It is much faster to dictate a letter into a machine than to write it out in longhand, and much easier than organising common time in which to give shorthand to a secretary. After each phone call you make or receive, you can pick up the machine and dictate a quick attendance note. In fact the machine is a necessity, but you should also be aware of its disadvantages.

At first you will feel very self-conscious using a dictaphone — your voice sounds odd when you play it back and you feel that everyone is listening while you fumble with the controls. This feeling soon passes, but even when you are more accomplished you should still be wary. The dictaphone is responsible for many badly written letters, which lose their structure and ramble repetitively. This is because the writer has lost his concentration and forgotten what he has already said. It is also because we speak differently from the way we write, and a letter composed as if the writer were talking will probably be very badly expressed.

To avoid these pitfalls, it is a good idea to plan the letter, to determine what you are going to say and the order in which you are going to say it. If you make brief notes on the main issues, you can then dictate from them. For example, if dictating a complex matter you may find tabulation helps to make your letter clearer. But decide on your headings and

sub-headings in advance and tell the secretary what you are doing.

When you dictate, remember how easy it is to misunderstand the spoken word, especially since the sound reproduction of the machines is not always very good. Speak clearly — if only to save your secretary having to ask half the office to listen to what you have said. Spell out names and unusual words.

Specify what punctuation you want, and when you want a new paragraph. Try to put yourself in your secretary's place and remember that she can't read your mind.

Before you start to dictate you should ensure that you have copies of all letters, files, addresses, and reference numbers on your desk so that you can quickly refer to them during the dictation. Liaise with your secretary to find out what documentation she would like accompanying the tape. In most cases it would probably be sensible to give your secretary the file and tape together. This way she can check relevant information and ensure the correct format is used.

When the letter is typed check it meticulously, because there is an even higher risk of mistakes when a letter is produced in this way.

Never allow a document or letter to be sent out unless you have carefully checked it yourself. If your pronounciation is unclear the typist may type her interpretation. If this is not checked it could have disastrous results. There is an anecdotal story of a typist who misinterpreted 'ipso facto' as 'if so fatso'.

To help your secretary further, tell her how much work there is on each tape and what files you have worked on, or write this on a 'sticky' and attach it to the tape. This enables her to organise her own time. But however organised she is, it is in the nature of things that she will have a backlog of work. So if a matter is genuinely urgent, put it on a separate

tape and tell her, so that it does not wait in the heap. Don't do this unless you really have to: the more often you do it, the less effect it will have.

WRITING LETTERS

Whenever you write, whether to a client or to another professional, you are trying to communicate. Hence you must think carefully about what you want to say and how best to say it, so that the recipient understands what you mean. You must use words accurately and in a style appropriate to the context and to the person who will read the letter. Your aims are clarity, comprehensibility and precision. Conciseness is also desirable, since bulky writing is difficult to read and therefore less efficient. Nevertheless, your letters must be complete, so conciseness may have to give way to precision. But remember, your client will not thank you for a five-page letter when half a page would have done — especially if he has to pay for it!

The best way to achieve these goals of clarity, comprehensibility and precision is to keep it short. This applies equally to words, sentences, paragraphs and whole letters. Every word should be there because you want it to be. Write critically, so that you cut out waffle and padding.

Psychologists have discovered that our understanding of what we read decreases sharply if there are more than twenty-five words in a sentence. However, you may find you need a long sentence. In this case you can help the reader by tabulating it. Consider the following examples:

'An agency relationship may be created by express agreement between the parties, by implied authorisation, where the agent has power to do everything within the usual scope of his business, and by estoppel, when someone has apparent authority to act as agent for another against a third party.'

'An agency relationship may be created by:
(a) express agreement between the parties, or
(b) implied authorisation, where the agent has power to do everything within the usual scope of his business, or
(c) estoppel, when someone has apparent authority to act as agent for another as against a third party.'

You probably found the second example easier to understand because the writer has done half the work for you. Equally, if a letter has to cover several different issues, consider making a numbered list of them. This will be easier to read and reply to since the recipient can simply refer to your numbers.

Resist the temptation to use long words in the hope that they will make you sound learned — a client may not understand them and you will just sound pompous. A sensible guideline is to use familiar words rather than legal jargon. A client is more likely to be impressed by your ability if you get him the result that he wants, and you are more likely to get his co-operation in achieving that result if he can understand what you are saying.

Before you start to write a letter, ask yourself why you are writing it, what you want to say in it and what you want the other party to understand from it. Until you have this clear in your own mind, you cannot possibly communicate to someone else. Think about your recipient and the style in which you can best communicate with him: is he another lawyer, a bank manager, a company client, a council house tenant who wishes to buy the house, or a distraught matrimonial client? They all have their different needs and your letter should be written appropriately. Even when writing to another lawyer there is no point in using long, technical words just for the sake of it. Similarly, Latin should be used with care. Such terms as 'res ipsa loquitur' may be useful shorthand between lawyers, but most clients will not understand them. Having decided what you want to say, plan the content into a logical format, so that you lead your reader logically through it.

As a lawyer you must use words precisely so they say exactly what you mean, clearly and unambiguously. So you must write critically, and after you have written, review what you have said. Remember, one day your letter may have to be read by a judge! It must convey information precisely, because your client may rely on it in making major decisions. If written on your client's instructions it must comply with them exactly, because it may (for example) form the basis of a binding contract. If there is anything wrong, revise the letter until it is accurate. It is said that there is no such thing as good writing, only good rewriting. If in doubt, take instructions from your client or advice from your principal.

Ask the secretary who does your work how much information she wants you to give her. For example, she may want the recipient's full name and address or she may be content to take these from the file. You may save yourself a lot of work and avoid irritating her by asking. You must certainly check letters when they have been typed. Never sign a letter in a hurry, e.g. because the post is about to go, without reading it through. It is your job, not that of the secretary, to ensure that the finished product says what you intended. If there is a mistake in a typed letter, have it corrected by the typist — this is easy enough with a word-processor — because letters corrected by hand look shoddy and give a bad impression. Make sure that the other party's reference is on the letter, so that it does not end its days lost in another firm's query tray. You should identify the subject-matter of the letter, e.g. 'Sale of No 1 Acacia Avenue'. Do you need 'Subject to contract' or 'Without prejudice' at the top? Have you made any undertakings? If so, do you have the client's authority to do so, and the consent of your principal? Be particularly careful with letters before action in litigation, and ensure that they state fully what you are claiming and on what grounds. This will be the first document the judge reads and will set the tone of the whole proceedings. It looks bad if you subsequently try to adopt a completely different line of attack.

In some common circumstances you can save yourself a lot of time by preparing stock letters. When you exchange contracts on your client's sale and purchase, for example, you simply ask a secretary to send out the standard letter, instead of having to write one from scratch. You may well find such letters are already widely used in your firm. Just check they are really appropriate to this client and these circumstances.

DRAFTING

Whenever you draft a legal document your task is to cater for all the client's needs clearly, precisely and without ambiguity. Ideally you should achieve this by using language which he can understand, but not if this means sacrificing precision. The document must be tailor-made to your client's needs and must deal with all possible contingencies. A well-drafted document means that if a dispute ever arises, the issue will already have been disposed of. To achieve this you must think round the problem and imagine all the eventualities which may arise. Your draft may have to regulate a relationship far into the future and stand the test of time. This is a lot to ask, but it is what the client is paying for.

The first stage is to take full, clear instructions from the client. Then you have to think long and hard about what the client really needs, and how best to achieve it. What form should the document take, for whom is it intended, how long must it last? Should it be impressively bulky or light so it is not too imposing? Is it to be used only once, will it be needed for a long time or used as a standard form? Is it to be read by laymen or lawyers? Only when you have thought this through can you decide whether to use a precedent, and if so which one. Your firm may have its own precedents, or you may use (for example) the *Encyclopaedia of Forms and Precedents*. If there is no suitable precedent, or if two precedents have to be merged, it is probably sensible in your early days in practice to ask an experienced draftsman for advice.

Once you have found a suitable precedent the tendency is to think either that you only need to fill in the gaps or that, because the precedent was produced by an experienced lawyer, every word of it must stay in. Neither is true. Precedents are simply detailed check-lists, to remind you of possibilities, risks and alternatives. Their annotations may put you on warning of relevant legal issues. But precedents should never be used slavishly. It is said that a precedent is a starting point, not an answer. Every clause must be considered critically, and left out if it is not necessary. Otherwise you produce a document which is only a vague approximation to your client's needs, and the danger (especially with the widespread use of word-processors) is that documents become ever longer.

Of course, such critical drafting needs experience and specialist knowledge. As a trainee solicitor you are bound to be wary before leaving clauses out, but the basic principle should be borne in mind. Similarly, you must check that the precedent is up to date, and check it for judicial definitions or legal restrictions — there is no point in including an excessive clause in restraint of trade which realistically leaves your client with no protection at all.

Your job is to produce a document which is concise and clear and caters precisely for your client's needs. The document should be self-defining and should clarify such problem areas as time limits. Different words should not be used to mean the same thing, since this is likely to lead to confusion: similarly, the same word should not be used to mean different things.

It may help to bear in mind that if your document ever ends up in court it will be interpreted according to the following established principles:

(1) The document will usually be read as a whole. The

courts are wary of admitting extrinsic evidence to show that the words were intended to have an unusual meaning.

(2) Any recitals or marginal notes may be used to find the meaning of the document.

(3) Words are given their ordinary, natural meaning unless you specify otherwise.

(4) If a clause is ambiguous it will be interpreted 'contra proferentem', i.e. strictly against the party seeking to rely on it.

(5) 'Expressio unius est exclusio altereus': express reference to one thing excludes others which are not specifically referred to. So do not include vast detail unless it is strictly necessary. If it is, make sure it is comprehensive.

(6) 'Euisdem generis': if a list of specific items forming a category is followed by a general clause, the general clause is taken to refer only to things within the same category.

(7) 'Noscitur a socus': words must be interpreted in context.

You even have to think about the presentation of the document. It should follow a logical order, using headings and sub-headings if they make it easier to read. Numbered, indented clauses, with an index, make a bulky document more manageable. Remember the advantages of tabulation to make complex clauses easier to understand. The process of breaking the clause down will also help you think more clearly about it. It is so easy to draft ambiguously because you have not thought of an alternative meaning. Also consider whether your draft would be clearer if you removed detail into schedules as the flow of the main document is undisturbed. For example, if you have many terms which need defining, a schedule may be more efficient than a definitions clause.

Precisely because drafting demands such intense concentration if done properly, many experienced draftsmen start with a pen and paper rather than a dictaphone: the process of writing encourages critical thought. Ideally, a first draft should be done in peace and quiet — use your diary to block out the necessary amount of time, away from the telephone and clients. Then leave it for a while, and preferably sleep on it, before revising it with a fresh mind.

When you do revise, check it critically. Read it as if you were the other side, looking for weaknesses. Is the terminology consistent? Is every clause necessary? Do *you* understand what you have written? If you don't, no-one else will. Is it clear who is supposed to do what, when, where? Check your use of pronouns because they are a fertile source of ambiguity. Is it absolutely clear which noun they refer to? In normal writing we use them to avoid unnecessary repetition of nouns. In technical drafting it is often safer to repeat the noun because precision is more important than elegance. Watch your use of punctuation. A comma in the wrong place can totally alter the sense of what you are saying. This is why traditionally technical documents are drafted without punctuation. This is a shame because it certainly makes documents more readable. But be wary. Remember, it is said that Roger Casement was hanged by a comma in the Statute of Treasons! If you are satisfied that the document is clear, number and date it. You should keep all your drafts on file as evidence of your thinking process and in case of later dispute, so numbering is necessary to avoid earlier drafts being mistaken for later ones.

Only after this thorough revision should you send two copies to the other side for amendment if this is appropriate. When you receive a draft, read it critically: it is bound to favour the draftsman's client. But don't amend for the sake of it — if a draft is adequate, do not feel you have to make red marks. When you get back an amended version of your own draft, check any amendments carefully in terms of your earlier thought processes and ensure that the terminology is consistent. If the draft keeps going backwards and forwards it might be sensible to arrange a meeting to resolve the dispute.

The process of drafting a document properly is such hard work and so time-consuming that there is a great temptation to use that draft as a precedent in the future. Yet this is clearly dangerous. All the work has been geared towards producing a document tailor-made for this client and carefully negotiated with the other side. You have excluded unnecessary clauses and varied others. If you then use this as a precedent, you risk omitting an essential clause or including one which is disastrous. Go back to the original precedent, the detailed check-list, which will remind you of the relevant issues.

INTERVIEWING CLIENTS

Recent reports on the legal profession have shown clearly that the major cause of discontent among clients is bad communication — and conversely that clients respond with gratitude when their solicitor does communicate with them well. In particular, the first interview with a new client is crucial in ensuring that the client gains a good impression of you and of the firm. Otherwise, he may not come back.

First interview

It is essential that you start the first interview well, because first impressions are so important. Remember that your client may well be apprehensive and nervous — he is in a strange environment, he has probably come to see you because he is worried about a problem, and he is also likely to be concerned about your bill. If you keep him waiting he may become even more edgy. He may also be annoyed at your rudeness and unimpressed by your lack of organisation.

Think about where you are going to interview the client. He will not be impressed by a cluttered room or a desk heaped with disorderly papers. Nor will he be pleased if his account of his problem is disturbed by the telephone. Hence it is often better to use an interview room which has no such distractions.

We all make decisions about one another within the first few minutes of meeting. Hence appearances are crucial, especially to a trainee solicitor who may himself lack confidence. If you look and behave like a solicitor, the client is more likely to believe in you. Make the client feel wanted by greeting him with a firm handshake and a smile. An offer of coffee will make him feel more welcome. Help to dispel his nerves by introducing yourself. Trainee solicitors often try to hide their status, feeling that the client will not have faith in anyone but a fully-fledged solicitor. This can lead to greater problems if the client later finds out the truth. Anyway, most clients will accept an explanation that you are in training and are under the supervision of an experienced solicitor. At least you won't be so expensive!

Invite the client to sit down, and help him relax by appearing relaxed yourself — attempts to look important will only make him more edgy. Ask him to tell you what the problem is, and listen to what he says. Listening is one of the essential skills of effective interviewing, and it is hard work. We tend to be lazy listeners. We hear what we expect to hear. We listen to the start and then assume we know what is to follow. We make assumptions based on our own experiences, which may be irrelevant. Instead of listening accurately, we plan what we are going to say in reply. This is dangerous because most people do not speak coherently, especially when they are worried or upset. You must hear what is said and notice what is not said. Is the account logical or jumbled? Even the client's gestures and tone of voice can tell you so much. Let him give you the basic outline in his own words and resist the temptation to interrupt, or to assume that you know what he is saying. Most clients do not speak sufficiently coherently for us to skim-listen. Yet lawyers are particularly at risk of doing so, because our training teaches us to look for legal pigeon-holes. As students we were given problems to discuss which clearly centred on particular legal issues. Real clients are usually less easy to classify.

We all feel offended if the person we are talking to is obviously not listening, so make your client feel wanted by showing you are interested. Look at him (without staring him out), and make encouraging noises to lead him on. We all like people who are like us. If you watch friends in a social setting they often adopt similar postures. This instinctive behaviour has lead to a technique called 'mirroring' which you can use to help the client relax. Without exaggerating, adopt his posture and gestures. In many cases this will help him feel at ease and more willing to talk to you. Of course you will have to make notes, but the danger is that in doing so you lose eye contact and the client thinks you are not listening. This can be avoided by telling the client what you are doing and why, and by trying to look at him as much as you can.

When you have heard his story, start asking questions to fill in the gaps, clarify the confusions and ascertain any other information you need. Only ask one question at a time. If you ask two or three together they are unlikely to be fully answered and you risk not being given all the information you need. You will usually gain more information and detail by using open questions, the ones which start with 'what', 'why', 'where', 'when', 'who', or 'how'. Closed questions, can usually only be answered 'yes' or 'no' — these are useful for keeping a talkative client on the right track. When you have asked a question, wait for the answer. We are all wary of silence and hence talk to fill it up. The risk is that we may not then hear what the client was about to say. By simply remaining silent you put pressure on the client to speak.

It is then useful to summarise your understanding of the position, listening carefully to any amendments your client makes and clarifying points which may be legally important. If you do not understand something that is said, ask. Don't just assume that it will become clear later because it may well not do so and then it will be too late to ask. A useful technique is to repeat or rephrase what the client has said, since he will usually then expand on it. This is a particularly useful method if the client is upset or you are unsure what he means. It also makes him feel you are really concentrating on what he is saying.

The client has probably come to you for advice, but in the first interview you are at a disadvantage because you do not know what the problem is and therefore have no chance to prepare. Advise the client if you are sure of your ground and you have your principal's authority to do so. If you do so, avoid long words and jargon — remember that your client is likely to be nervous and is more likely to understand simple, familiar words. If you are not sure of your ground, say that you wish to check up on the position. The danger is that trainee solicitors sometimes feel this is a sign of weakness, and try to bluster through. The client would prefer you to give him sound advice, even if he has to wait for it — and your firm certainly would.

Before you end the interview, summarise your advice, your opinion or what is going to be done. Precisely because clients tend to be edgy, they often do not take on board what you say. So emphasise what you are going to do and what, if anything, the client should do.

Many trainee solicitors find it difficult to discuss money with the client. You must remember that you are in a business, and also that the client is entitled to know where he stands. So consider whether he qualifies for legal aid, and, if not, follow your principal's guidelines about taking money on account of costs.

Lastly you must make a good final impression, since this is what the client goes away remembering. Ask him if he has any doubts or queries, and encourage him to contact you if anything occurs to him later, before you see him out and say goodbye. Don't leave him wandering around the corridors on his own.

The first thing you do after he has gone is to make a detailed attendance note of what you were told, what advice you gave, who is going to do what, and how long the discussion took. It is then sensible to confirm any important advice in a letter. This acts as a record of what you have said and makes the position absolutely clear to the client.

Common interviewing mistakes, and how to avoid them

The first interview is particularly difficult because you have little chance to prepare your ground. You may have only the scantiest idea of what the client's problem involves. If the client has already been seen by you or someone else in the firm, you are in a stronger position because you have the chance to prepare. This helps you stay in control of the interview and thus boosts your confidence. Remember that your comparative inexperience always makes you slightly vulnerable. If you do not prepare properly, you are far more likely to make mistakes and bear the brunt of the client's criticism. Generally he will accept it if you do not feel you can advise him, but he is entitled to expect you to know his position. So give yourself time to read the file carefully, check that everything has been done that needs to be done, and give yourself time to research any necessary material so that you are sure of your ground and have anticipated any likely questions. If appropriate, find out about the client's business so you can view things from his perspective and speak his language. A frequent criticism from commercial clients is that lawyers do not understand what they are about.

You may even wish to prepare a check-list of points you want to clarify and information you need to help you keep in control of the interview. Work out in advance what the client really needs, and how best you can help him. Many experienced solicitors have standard form check-lists which they pin to the front of the file. By ticking things off as they are done they ensure nothing is forgotten.

Preparation even extends to checking that you are appropriately dressed, and that the interview room is laid out in a manner which will encourage the client to give you the information you need. The medical profession, for example, has long realised that a desk can be a barrier which makes the interviewee feel inferior and therefore unwilling to talk. You may even have to remember to book the room in advance.

Be careful not to pigeon-hole the client. As mentioned above, lawyers are trained to analyse a situation so as to find the legal issue within it. The real-life problems that clients bring you are usually much more complex, often raising many different issues. If you rush to a preliminary view, you risk missing other essentials and therefore giving your client inadequate advice. You must listen to the full story carefully, and only then consider the full range of legal possibilities and available remedies. In addition, the legal position may be only one relevant factor: emotional, commercial or other considerations may be just as (or more) important.

Lawyers often forget the elementary social graces. This is not only rude but also inefficient. If you shake hands with the client, smile at him and welcome him, he is more likely to relax. If he feels that you are friendly he will be more willing to give you the information you need. As a result, the interview will be more effective and proceed more smoothly. Aggressive questioning is likely to make him clam up. Similarly it is counter-productive to assume a self-important pose, because this may well intimidate the client. It is easy to underestimate how much impact we have on clients through non-verbal behaviour. Open hand gestures and eye contact will usually make a client feel relaxed. In contrast he is likely to feel you are being defensive if you cross your arms, or arrogant and superior if you lean back in your chair with your hands behind your head.

You must ensure that your client understands what is happening in his case and what you are doing for him. If he does not, he is likely to ring you to find out — probably when it is least convenient to you. This is why it is so important to summarise at the end of an interview, and to do so in clear, simple English. This does not mean you have to be patronising: lawyers do tend to use jargon without even realising it. Of course, clients' levels of knowledge vary, but the essence of communication is to think about this recipient and what is appropriate to him. You should always end the interview by telling the client what you plan to do, what he should do, and whether you will be contacting him (and if so when) or you will wait for him to contact you.

Always remember that you are there to advise your client and then to carry out his instructions. You must obtain his agreement before doing anything on his behalf. If he says he does not plan to follow your advice, you should check with your principal and confirm your advice in writing. If anything goes wrong later there will be documentary evidence of what you suggested.

Always be on the look-out for conflicts of interest, e.g. if your firm is instructed to act for both parties in a conveyancing transaction. Consider the Law Society guidelines and ask for your principal's advice. Similarly, if you are involved in a litigation matter remember the particular responsibilities of the solicitor as an officer of the Supreme Court. Certainly he has a duty to do his best for his client, but he must never deceive or mislead the court. Nor may he withhold information to which the court is entitled; he must, for example, disclose any relevant decisions even if they do not assist his client's case. If the client admits that he has committed perjury, the solicitor must refuse to act further in those proceedings unless the client fully discloses his perjury to the court.

Finally, beware of becoming personally involved. This is not to say you should become callous and cynical, but as soon as you become emotionally involved in a case you lose your objectivity and your judgment. Yet this is precisely what your client is paying you for, and the only real way you can help him.

TAKING WITNESS STATEMENTS

If interviewing clients can be tricky, extracting information from witnesses is potentially even more difficult. Remember, there is usually nothing in it for them in giving the statement — they are just being helpful, and are involving themselves in a lot of trouble and the risk of a court attendance by doing so. Hence courtesy is of paramount importance.

It is usually a good idea to start by writing to a witness whom you wish to interview. Explain who you are acting for and why you would like to talk to him. Since the witness would be doing you and your client a favour by seeing you, you cannot assume that he will be willing to visit your office. This may be just too much trouble, and he may decide not to help at all. You should therefore offer to visit him at his convenience, possibly even in the evening or at the weekend.

When you see the witness, all the normal guidelines to good interviewing apply. You must be friendly and make him feel welcome. Most importantly, you must listen carefully and precisely to what he says. Remember that everyone sees something different in any given situation, and you must be on the look-out for any inconsistencies. For this reason, you should have your client's proof of evidence in front of you so that you can check what the witness does and does not agree with. This may be crucial if the matter later goes to court.

If possible make a full, written statement as you interview the witness; then ask him to read it, and sign and date it at the end. A typed copy may be sent to him later, together with a stamped, addressed envelope for its return. If anything happens to him in the meantime, at least you will have the manuscript copy. If this is not practicable, at least dictate the statement in his presence so that he can correct anything which is wrong.

Witnesses often ask whether they are obliged to give you a statement. You have to be honest and admit that they are not. Remember also that there is no property in a witness: he is free to speak to the other side if he so wishes, although they are not entitled to demand a copy of your statement.

Witnesses sometimes fear that if they give a statement they will have to go to court. Again, you have to be honest and admit that this is possible (though they may still have to go to court even if they *don't* give a statement). However it may help if you explain where the case will be held and who will be there. If, for example, the issue is being dealt with by an industrial tribunal, you can soothe the witness' anxiety by pointing out that the proceedings will be less formal than a court hearing. You can also point out that of every 100 actions begun only one reaches trial, and even then many possible witnesses are not called. The Supreme Court rules permit the court to order exchange of witness evidence before trial in some actions. This should cut down even further the number of cases reaching trial, and should make hearings shorter and cheaper by reducing the number of witnesses called.

At the end of the interview, again remember the basic courtesies; thank the witness for his time and trouble. As soon as possible afterwards make a detailed attendance note, which should include your assessment of the witness. Another lawyer may deal with the matter in court, and your opinion as to the witness' reliability and likely confidence under questioning may be invaluable.

Basic principles of witness statements

The use of witness statements in still in its infancy (RSC, Order 38, rule 2A).

If the witness statement is to be used at the trial it must contain all the evidence the witness will wish to give in chief. Do not anticipate what will be required during cross-examination.

The witness statement can only be related to issues of fact which the witness is able to prove of his own knowledge. It must be the truth, the whole truth and nothing but the truth and must not contain inadmissible evidence. It should not contain hearsay or expressions of belief.

Make sure that every point in your pleaded case is covered.

Form of the witness statement

The witness statement should be expressed in the first person and should state the full name, address and occupation of the witness. It must also state whether he is a party and in what capacity he is called.

The statement should be treated as evidence in chief and regarded as if you gave the evidence in the witness box.

It should be in clear and narrative form, in the words of the witness. It should be chronological.

The statement should be divided into numbered paragraphs each dealing with a separate topic.

The dates and numbers should be in figures. It should be typed double-spaced on one side only.

It is good practice to sign and date the statement and to witness the signature.

USING COUNSEL

Instructing counsel

You may instruct counsel for a variety of reasons, e.g. to act as an advocate, to draft pleadings or other documents, or simply to give advice. In any event, the solicitor owes a professional duty to his client and he cannot escape this merely by instructing counsel. If he does decide to do so he must ensure that the barrister he selects is competent to do the job. To instruct inexperienced counsel in a matter where this is not appropriate may in any event prove more expensive in the long run. The choice of counsel is often based on experience, on knowing who has done a good job in the past or which chambers specialise in what area. Your principal's advice can be invaluable here. Remember that the barrister's clerk is not impartial. He will try to make sure that you get the right person for the sake of goodwill, but he will give you anyone rather than turn work away.

It is your duty to provide counsel with adequate instructions, and all relevant documentation, in good time. It is unprofessional to send counsel a bundle of correspondence with such instructions as 'Counsel has all relevant papers and is asked to advise'. It is your job to give him the information he needs. Indeed many barristers refuse to accept such vague instructions because it means that the solicitor is not doing his job. He has met the client and ought to know his way around the file. It is a waste of time and money to expect counsel to sort it all out for himself, and you (or your client) will end up paying for it — if not in terms of the fee, then in terms of the time which counsel can spend on the work that actually needs to be done.

What you should do is to outline the main facts and the issues involved, referring to all relevant correspondence and documentation. You can help counsel by drawing his attention to any issues which are not immediately obvious or which particularly concern you. It is tactful to do this in such a way as to avoid suggesting (even if it is true) that you suspect he might not otherwise notice the point in question — e.g. 'Counsel will be aware that . . . .' The clearer the information you give about your requirements, the more likely it is that they will be met. If you want counsel to advise, specify as precisely as possible what questions you want answered, as well as asking him to 'advise generally'.

If possible, agree the fee with counsel's clerk in advance. Unless you are going to pay straight away, the instructions should state clearly that the fee will be paid at the conclusion of the proceedings. In legal aid matters, the backsheet should be marked 'Legal Aid' and the bundle should include a copy of the legal aid certificate — but check first that it covers the cost of instructing counsel! As soon as you deliver instructions your firm is liable for counsel's fees, so do not do so without authority. The backsheet should also identify counsel, the instructing solicitors and the name of the proceedings or matter.

If you ask counsel to draft documents such as pleadings, it is your duty to check them when they come back to you. There may be silly mistakes like incorrect dates or names. Check that everything necessary is pleaded. If you fail (e.g.) to ask for interest, or to allege contributory negligence, the court may refuse to order in your favour; and even if you are allowed to amend, you will be responsible for any additional costs. Any apparent errors or inconsistencies should be drawn to counsel's attention. You may even need to take further advice.

Conferences and court attendances

The client generally cannot go to a barrister direct, and it is still true that the barrister should not see the client (except perhaps a professional client) in the absence of the instructing solicitor. Whenever there is a conference or a court hearing, therefore, a representative from the instructing solicitor's office must be present. This often falls to the lot of the trainee solicitor, who may be bewildered as to what he is supposed to do.

Start by reading the file carefully (if you have time). Counsel may be in charge of the case, but you represent his instructing solicitors and he is entitled to expect you to have some idea what is going on. At a conference your job is to make full notes, since counsel's oral advice is not normally confirmed in writing.

The first time you go to court you may be thrown by the simple problem of where to find your barrister, especially if you have not already met him. If there are barristers already in the court where your case is due to be heard, ask one of the ushers. They are immensely helpful and will usually know which of the bewigged figures is yours — or will help you find out. Alternatively, if there are barristers milling about outside the court you can call out something like 'Is Mr Rumpole here please?' If this doesn't work either, ask at reception for a call to be put out for him over the public address system.

Counsel cannot speak to witnesses (except expert witnesses) at all, even in the presence of his instructing solicitors. So one of your jobs is to settle them down in the waiting-room (if any) and tell them what is happening. In a

criminal trial they may not go into court before giving evidence — in a civil case they normally can. If in doubt, ask counsel.

You may of course find that another of your tasks is to explain to a bewildered client why a barrister is necessary anyway. He has probably come to put his trust in you (or more likely your principal) and may object to paying extra for another lawyer who does not know the case so well.

In court you sit on the bench behind your barrister. You need to be near him in case he needs your help or you need to convey information to him. The client should sit near you if there is room, for similar reasons (unless of course he is in the dock). Stand up when the judge enters or leaves, and bow when everybody else does. If you have to leave the room during the case, do so quietly and bow to the judge as you leave and as you return. He will ignore you. (If he doesn't, you weren't quiet enough.) Never even *move* while anyone is taking the oath.

Your main role in court is to make notes of what is said, especially when it is impossible for counsel to do so because he is on his feet. This is so even if there is an official shorthand writer in court, because counsel needs to have his own record of the evidence as a basis for later questions and for his closing speech. The note required may (depending on the circumstances) be anything from a bare summary to a verbatim, blow-by-blow account. It is worth taking a full note of submissions by counsel for the other side, but it is reasonable to assume that your counsel knows what his own submissions are. Observations made by the judge are always important. There is usually no need to write out the evidence of a witness who simply repeats his proof of evidence, but note down any discrepancies. Cross-examination should be copied down as fully as possible: if it is impossible to get down the questions as well as the answers, write down the answers in such a way as to *include* the questions. Keeping up is easier than it sounds, because the judge will also be making notes and will soon ask counsel to slow down if necessary. Use a counsel's notebook if possible: your firm may not have them, but counsel will. Write only on the right-hand pages, leaving the left ones blank for notes. If in doubt, find a convenient moment to ask counsel. But do not use a tape recorder without express permission.

Afterwards, counsel will congratulate or commiserate with the client as appropriate. Make sure you get him to explain the outcome if you are not sure. If the judge makes an order, write it down and check with counsel that you have got it right. Don't assume that you can ring and ask him later: even if you manage to get hold of him, he won't remember. Apologise for being obtuse if you like, but make sure he tells you what you need to know. You may feel a fool asking these questions in front of the client, but you will feel more of a fool if he (or your principal) asks you later and you don't know.

PUBLIC SPEAKING

Perhaps surprisingly, the most common human fear is not of death, bereavement, war, flying or even a close encounter with a hairy spider — it is of having to speak in public. However, this is a skill essential to practice as a solicitor. If you are a litigant, you will of course have to develop advocacy skills, but increasingly even non-litigious solicitors are having to present client seminars or 'beauty parades'.

The problem is that as soon as you get nervous you shake, you feel sick, your palms go sweaty and your brain refuses to function. So to do the job effectively you must learn to control your nerves. There are several techniques which can help.

The problem is that your body has automatically gone into 'fight or flight' response. At a very basic level it has perceived a danger and has pumped adrenaline into your system so you are ready to protect yourself. Unfortunately, the result is unhelpful in this context. For physiological reasons, deep breathing helps to calm your system down. Other well-known relaxation techniques will also help. Master them in advance so you can use them easily when you need them. Also check how you are programming yourself. Are you telling yourself that you are going to make a mess of the presentation? Are you convinced you are going to forget what you want to say? If you are, you will.

You can have faith in yourself because you are going to prepare thoroughly. This is another method of controlling stress and boosting your confidence. You must decide why you are making the speech — if you are not sure, your audience won't be. Then give yourself time to research your material so that you are happy with it.

Find out about your audience. Your style will be very different if you are talking to colleagues or to clients. Can you assume any understanding? Is technical jargon appropriate? Is your message likely to be controversial?

Anticipate objections and other views so that you are less likely to be thrown. Then organise your material with a clear, logical format which is easy to follow and appropriate to your audience. Some material has its own logic. For example, if you are giving a lecture on economic loss, recent court decisions provide you with a structure. Other subjects may be more amorphous so you must think through your material carefully. Make sure the format is clear in your own mind so you have confidence on the day. Bear in mind how difficult it is to listen. We all have a very short span of concentration and are easily distracted. Your audience will be grateful if you help them by structuring your speech, telling them what the structure is and then sticking to it. Finally, give yourself a chance to rehearse — verbatim in front of a mirror if necessary. This is the best way to tell how long your talk will take, and it will boost your confidence to know that you have done it once already.

On the day, arrive in good time. you will not start well if you are harassed, flustered and hot. You will need time before the presentation to relax. You also need to check the room layout. If appropriate you may want to move furniture. For example, if you are talking to a group of a dozen people and you want to provoke a discussion, they are more likely to respond if they are sitting facing each other rather than behind one another. You may also need time to check equipment. If you are using an overhead projector, make sure your slides can be seen from the back of the room. If you are using a television, check in advance it is working. If you are showing a video, ensure you know how to use the machine. There are few things worse than fighting unknown gadgetry in front of a restive audience.

Make sure your dress is appropriate: this wins your audience's confidence and boosts your own morale. You will feel very silly if you are wearing denim jeans while lecturing to an audience of bank managers all of whom are wearing pin-striped suits. Decide in advance whether you want to sit or stand while speaking. It is generally easier to listen to someone who is standing. However, if you are speaking to a small group, sitting makes the presentation more informal. It is much more friendly if you say who you are — no-one wants to listen to an anonymous robot. Start by getting their attention and explaining clearly what you are going to talk about. Tell them what the structure of your talk is going to be, and then follow it. If you have said that you have five main points, flag each one as you make it and then summarise it before moving on to the next. When you have made all your points, draw your conclusions and stop neatly. Never dribble to a close, and never speak for longer than you said you would — that is breaking the contract.

You may find that key cards, or a list of prompting words, help you to remember the content of your speech — but never read from notes. It is impossible to listen to anyone who has his head buried in a file. If you do lose your train of thought, don't panic. Keep in control and calmly look at your notes. Your audience will not notice unless you fluster; what seems like an age of silence to you will simply be a natural pause to them. Eye contact with your audience is essential, because it makes you seem friendly and human and therefore easier to listen to. Vary your style, your gestures and your tone of voice — you know how much difference this makes

when you are listening to someone else. Visual aids may be useful if they genuinely add to your message, but don't use too many and don't use them for the sake of it. They can be very distracting if used inappropriately. And never rely on them — Murphy's Law of Technology state that the likelihood of its going wrong is in direct proportion to the chaos which will ensue if it does.

Researchers in the area of public speaking have concluded that a speaker makes far more impact on his audience by his body language and vocal quality than by the content of what he says. This is why it is so important to look at your audience, to smile at them and to make open, welcoming gestures. Try to avoid crossing your arms while talking. This is perceived by most people as a defensive barrier even though you may not mean it as such. This is also why many lecturers do not use a lectern in case they are perceived as hiding behind it. Variety, openness, volume and clarity make you credible; formality and uniformity have the reverse effect. Your listeners can think about three times as fast as you can speak, so you must constantly work at keeping their attention. You will quickly lose it if you repeat the same stimuli, so use stories, examples, metaphors and pictures to add interest and make what you say more memorable. If appropriate, involve the audience by encouraging them to participate. This takes some courage, but it is much more fun for them. Your listeners need variety, are attracted by enthusiasm and are compelled by a smile. This is difficult when you are scared, because the temptation is to become aggressive and confrontational; but you are much safer if your audience like you. Make them feel wanted and maintain their interest; watch their responses and vary your style accordingly. Their positive reactions will make your confidence soar.

APPLICATIONS BEFORE DISTRICT
JUDGES OR MASTERS

Such applications often fall to the lot of the trainee solicitor, who is immediately at a disadvantage because he does not know the ropes. The general points made about effective speaking apply equally here.

Again the emphasis is on preparation. The best of advocates will fail if he is not familiar with the papers. You should receive the documentation a few days before the hearing and you should read it then. Do not leave it until the last minute, because you must check everything is in order — that, for example, the summons and affidavits have been served. If there is anything wrong, you must chase it up. But to be able to do so, you must first read the file and read it critically so that you do spot any lurking defects.

Check what the summons seeks, and look at the relevant court rules to see what orders the court can make. You will feel much safer at the hearing if you know your way around the rules, especially if your opponent is floundering. Read the correspondence and affidavits, so that you know which facts are in dispute and can quickly find the points you need. Such familiarity suggests efficiency, and will impress a busy district judge or master much more than the person who has to shuffle through mounds of paper to find what he needs. If your argument is complex, make a list of the important points you wish to raise, and use it as a memory aid while you speak. A chronology of events may also help, and may

be circulated at the hearing to the benefit of all concerned. Anticipate the outcome. If you are asking for summary judgment for a debt, work out the interest before you go to the hearing. If the district judge finds in your favour, you can tell him your figures, thus avoiding a lot of frenzied activity with calculators. Remember, district judges are busy people and are grateful for anything which eases their workload.

On the day of the hearing, give yourself plenty of time to get to court. This is partially to help yourself. You are probably going to be nervous anyway — you can do without being rushed and harassed as well. It will help if you have time to compose yourself. It is also rude to keep other people waiting, since this suggests that you think your time is more valuable than theirs. In the case of a court, where time is highly pressurised, this is patently not the case. If you do turn up late you may find that your application has suffered at the hands of an annoyed registrar and that you have to explain to the client why this has happened. Take the relevant court rule book (e.g. the *County Court Practice*, or 'Green Book') with you. Your opponent may refer to a particular rule and you will be at a major disadvantage if you do not have it in front of you.

A major worry amongst trainee solicitors on a first hearing is that they simply do not know who does what, or even how to refer to people. A master is addressed as 'Master', a district judge as 'Sir' or 'Madam' (or 'Ma'am', pronounced 'Mam' as in 'ham'). The party making the application usually introduces himself and his opponent, making it clear who is acting for which client. He then briefly outlines the nature of the application, e.g. 'This is an application by the plaintiff for an interim payment of £10,000 on account of damages'. If affidavits have been filed in advance, the applicant should ask whether the district judge has had time to read them — if not, he should pause while

92

this is done. He will then put forward his arguments, relating them to the affidavits when this is helpful. The other party will make notes during the applicant's argument of any issues he wants to raise when he has his right of reply. Similarly the applicant will note any matters he wants to raise when his opponent has finished.

While you are talking, remember that the district judge is both busy and human. He will respond to a clear, logical argument. So do not waffle, or labour your points, just make them clearly and concisely. If you have one good point, make it and then stop — do not clutter it up with a lot of weak ones. If you succeed, remember to ask for costs, and a special allowance if the matter was complex. If you have used counsel, he may need reminding to ask for a certificate.

After the hearing, make a careful and complete note of the decision in case you need to appeal. Also make a detailed attendance note for the file. A county court draws up the order itself, but in the Queen's Bench Division the applicant is responsible for drawing and serving the order.

NEGOTIATION

Negotiation is a part of everyday life, although it is rarely thought of as such. We bargain with members of our household over who can have the car, who can watch which television programme, who helps with the washing-up. We negotiate with colleagues at work over who is to be responsible for what; we engage in a very subtle form of dealing when we buy a car or a house.

Equally, such dealing is central to many areas of legal practice. We negotiate when we settle a personal injury claim or a contract dispute, and many lawyers consider that the resolution of most matrimonial property arguments is not a matter of law at all.

Any conflict may be resolved by either persuasion or negotiation. The difference is that while persuasion seeks to make one party abandon his wishes completely, the goal of negotiation is to agree on a course of action which will partially satisfy the needs of both parties. Negotiation is a discussion between equals with a view to achieving a compromise which is acceptable to both, and from which each may even gain. Hence it is a process of obtaining concessions which totally or largely compensate for what you have given up. It is nothing to do with dogmatism, aggression or bullying.

To do this successfully, and represent your client's interests properly, thorough preparation is essential. You must know what the disputed issues are, what your

instructions are, why you are there and what you are trying to do. You must have clear in your mind what you *must* achieve, and what you would *like* to achieve. You must know your facts, and as much as possible about your opponent. You must anticipate his views and what his goals are likely to be. You must consider the possible variables and options, so that you can offer things of value to the other party in return for concessions that *you* value.

A common mistake is to assume that because something is not important to you, the other side will not value it. As a result you give it away cheaply. Consider the situation from their perspective and think about what you can give which is cheap to you but valuable to them. For example, the sale of a house may be very price-sensitive, both parties being on a tight budget. But you may reach an agreement if the vendor is prepared to leave the carpets, which are useless to him but save the purchaser enormous expense.

You should consider what information you can give and what you need. Research the background to the negotiation and think about the alternatives to agreement. When you are under pressure in a meeting it is easy to feel you have to reach agreement, however expensive this is. Having the cost of the alternatives clearly in mind will help you keep a sense of perspective. You should even spend time deciding where the meeting should be — your office, the office of the other solicitors or neutral ground: location and even the layout of the room will affect how you behave. Think about when the meeting is to be and choose a time when you will be at your best. If you are negotiating in a team, decide what roles you are going to take. Who is going to argue and who is going to listen? Do you need secretarial support to take minutes? All this preparation takes some pressure off you in the meeting itself so you can concentrate fully on the discussion.

This should prepare you to reach an agreement with

which you are both satisfied. Things can go badly wrong when parties take entrenched positions, demanding a specific deal, since the discussion is likely to become acrimonious. They are also likely to become committed to their position, so movement towards agreement is slow and expensive. This can be avoided if both parties look at their real interests and decide what they want rather than taking a forced position. It also helps if the discussion is based on objective criteria, e.g. current market values, precedents or professional standards. Lawyers are taught to criticise and analyse, but this is a weakness in negotiation. It is better to push ideas forward and consider them constructively. It may be possible to mix and match several ideas to produce a solution.

The most difficult task is often to keep control of yourself if you are negotiating with someone who is being unreasonable. Try to separate personalities from the discussion and treat the other side with courtesy so you can work together. They should be involved in the agreement as any deal you impose on them is unlikely to be implemented. Listen to what they say and summarise your understanding so you emphasise areas of agreement rather than difference.

Most negotiations follow a pattern, of which it may be helpful for you to be aware. First there is the introduction, the opening remarks which set the broad context. The next stage is an examination of differences, when the parties weigh each other up and indicate their positions. At the end of this, each party should know what the other wants and what he is prepared to give. The parties then try to move their positions closer by making proposals, before deciding whether they can trade concessions so as to reach an agreement. At this stage each should be aware not only of what a concession costs him, but of what it is worth to the other side. If the negotiation is successful, when the final agreement is made both parties should be satisfied that a fair resolution of the dispute has been reached.

Researchers have concluded that skilled negotiators constantly ask questions in order to control the discussion and to glean information. They listen as well as talk. They check regularly, by summarising and testing understanding, that both parties agree to what has been negotiated. When an agreement is reached, it is always carefully recorded in writing to avoid misunderstanding. Skilled negotiators are careful to avoid such emotive and irritating phrases as 'a generous offer' or 'a reasonable proposal', which achieve nothing positive and merely annoy the other side. They favour receptiveness to the other's proposals, instead of defensive aggression which is likely to inflame the relationship. Above all, they agree with one of the main rules of advocacy: if you have one good argument, stick to it — do not dilute it with four weaker arguments.

Negotiation is a highly skilled art, often consisting of complex and subtle manoeuvring between the parties in order to reach a satisfactory conclusion. But it is worth the trouble, because at the end the dispute is resolved and neither party is left embittered. Also, in a legal context, all the expense, wear and tear of a court hearing are avoided. During your articles, take the opportunity to watch experienced negotiators closely, and see how they apply these basic principles so as to achieve their result.

LEGAL RESEARCH

One of the jobs you are most likely to be given, even (or especially) in your early days with your firm, is that of researching points of law. Senior staff seldom have time for research; on the other hand the point may be too small, or too urgent, to send to counsel. Who better to do such a job than the new recruit, who may not know one end of a file from the other but is at least supposed to know something about the law?

The flaw in this reasoning, of course, is that learning about the law is a very different thing from learning how to find it. During your academic studies you were probably directed by your lecturers to the materials you needed to read. You may never have had to find the law for yourself. Don't panic: it isn't hard. You just need to get acquainted with a few basic tools.

First you need to familiarise yourself with the whereabouts, contents and layout of your firm's library. It may not be a separate room at all: sometimes the books are just distributed around the offices. But you must know where to find the materials that you are most likely to need in a hurry. Don't wait until you *are* in a hurry before you start finding your bearings.

Bear in mind that, as usual, accuracy is crucial. Make sure that you get every reference *exactly* right. If you copy out a quotation, get it right — down to the last comma. Above all, make sure that the conclusions you come up with are

relevant to the period in question. This may well mean that they must represent the law right now, but not necessarily: it depends on the problem. A lot of the work of solicitors (e.g. much tax work, and most litigation) concerns events which occurred some time ago, and which are therefore governed ·not by the law currently in force but by the law which *was* in force at the time in question. Have you ever sighed in exasperation when a lecturer told you about a statutory provision and then added that it had been repealed? Now you know better.

Textbooks and encyclopaedias

So where do you start to look? It depends what sort of query you have. If you have no pointers such as the names of relevant cases or legislation, but you simply need to find out the law on a particular point, you could start with a good, recent textbook on the subject in question. Practitioners' texts obviously tend to be more 'practical' in their approach than academic ones: what this means is that they are more likely to give you the fine detail as well as (or possibly instead of) the general principles.

The disadvantage of the traditional textbook is that it is several months out of date before it is even published, and then becomes increasingly unhelpful — if not downright misleading — until a supplement or a new edition appears. For this reason it is a good idea to consult one of the looseleaf works which are now available on almost every imaginable area of law. These works are supposed to be kept reasonably up to date by the regular issue of additional and/or replacement pages which are inserted according to the publishers' instructions. Whether you can rely on them depends whether the job of inserting the new pages is done promptly and efficiently — which you can ascertain to some extent by discreetly finding out who does it. (You may of course find that you get the job yourself, in which case you can at least ensure that it *is* done properly.)

If you can't find a suitable text on the area you want, or if you want to double-check, turn to what is perhaps the most useful single publication in the library: *Halsbury's Laws of England*. This is a huge and regularly updated encyclopaedia of the whole of English law. The current edition is the fourth. To make the most of it you need to be methodical:

(1) First look up the subject you want in the main index: this gives you a volume number (in bold type) and a paragraph number within that volume.

(2) Find the volume and turn to the appropriate paragraph.

(3) Don't spend hours reading it just yet, in case it is out of date. How can you tell? Find the *Cumulative Supplement* (make sure it is the latest one — 'cumulative' means it replaces all the earlier ones) and see if there is an entry for the volume and paragraph you have just looked at. If so, it will give you more recent information.

(4) Even the *Cumulative Supplement* only takes you up to the end of last year. For developments in the last few months, find the looseleaf binder entitled *Current Service* and check the 'Key' section at the front. If your volume and paragraph number appear there, it will give you a reference to either the Monthly Reviews or the Noter-up — both can be found further on in the binder. (Very often you will find nothing relevant in the *Current Service*, but don't fall into the trap of assuming that there will be nothing there. One day there will, and you'll be sorry.)

If you happen to know which volume contains the subject you want, you don't need to bother with the main index: go straight to that volume and consult the index devoted to the subject in question.

Legislation

Textbooks and encyclopaedias will of course refer you to relevant legislation as well as case law, but if you particularly want to find the legislation on a particular subject it is quicker to use *Halsbury's Statutes of England*. This is organised rather like the *Laws*, but instead of a full explanation of the law on each subject it gives you the text of the legislation relevant to that subject, with brief notes on repeals, amendments, case law etc. The procedure is:

(1) Use the index to find the volume which includes the subject you want. When you find some legislation which seems relevant to your problem, note the page number.
(2) Look under the appropriate volume and page number in the latest *Cumulative Supplement* and in the looseleaf *Noter-up Service*. This may give you further references to other volumes or to the looseleaf *Current Statutes Service*.

The disadvantage of this arrangement is that some statutes deal with more than one subject and therefore have to be distributed around several volumes. If you know which statute you want, it may be easier to find your way around it if you use one of the publications which keep each statute in one piece, e.g. *Current Law Statutes Annotated* or *Butterworth's Annotated Legislation Service*.

Wherever you find the legislation you want, *always* check on its subsequent history — i.e. whether it has been brought into force, repealed, amended or judicially considered, and whether any statutory instruments have been made under it. You can do all this with *Halsbury's Statutes*; or you can consult the latest *Current Law Legislation Citator*, together with the Statute Citator in the looseleaf binder entitled *Current Law Statutes*. (In theory you ought to finish the job by checking the last few issues of the monthly *Current Law*, but in practice they are usually sitting in somebody's in-tray.) A quick way of checking whether a provision is in force is the booklet *Is it in force?*, published as part of *Halsbury's Statutes*. It needs to be used together with the 'Is it in force?' section of the *Noter-up Service*. There is also a table of 'Legislation not yet in force' in the *Current Law Statutes* service.

For delegated legislation, the best source is usually *Halsbury's Statutory Instruments*. Again this is organised by subject, and you can find the volume you need by consulting the *Consolidated Index*. Check whether the information is up to date by consulting the *Annual Cumulative Supplement* and the *Monthly Survey-Key*.

Case law

You can usually find plenty of case law on a given point in *Halsbury's Laws,* and if you follow the procedure outlined above you should be able to find out whether any of the cases mentioned have been reversed, overruled or considered in later cases. Alternatively you can look up a particular case in the *Indexes to the Law Reports* or in the *Current Law Case Citator*. Very recent case law should be in the monthly *Current Law* — look in the Cumulative Case Citator section of the latest issue you can lay your hands on.

LEXIS

LEXIS, in case you have not encountered it, is an electronic database of legal information which can be consulted (at a price) via a computer terminal. It makes some forms of legal research much quicker, especially finding the current wording of much-amended legislation. It is also possible to get the text of cases which may not be in the library. Your firm may or may not have a terminal. If there is one, you will need authorisation before you can use it. You will also need training, if you have not already had it, and lots of practice. LEXIS is an additional research tool, not a substitute for all the others. By all means learn to use it if you have the chance, but learn to use the library first.

KEEPING UP TO DATE

You have probably just finished your formal legal education (doubtless with a sigh of relief). Nevertheless it is important that you keep your knowledge up to date. You cannot understand what your principal is doing or, more importantly, advise clients properly unless you know the current state of the law — and if you once let your knowledge slide, it takes a lot of effort to catch up.

Keeping up to date is a formidable task. There is such a vast amount of material published, it is impossible to keep abreast of all new developments. Virtually every practising solicitor appreciates that he may be out of date or may have missed some important recent development. You will never to manage to keep abreast of every development. However, the following points will ensure that you are kept reasonably up to date:

(1) Regularly and carefully read at least one legal journal, for example the *Law Society's Gazette*, the *Solicitors Journal,* the *New Law Journal* etc. This will ensure that you are at least aware of major developments in many areas of the law and keep up to date with developments within the profession.

(2) You will get a good outline of recent developments by checking one of the digests such as *Current Law,* Longman's *Busy Solicitors Digest* or CLT's *Legal Update.*

(3) Having identified which magazine you wish to read regularly, and referred to *Current Law* or one of the other digests, you will still find that there is a vast amount of other material which is relevant to you. However, you will undoubtedly find that you will not have time to read through all the other journals. What you should do is to photocopy (or get your secretary to photocopy) the contents page of specialist journals and other magazines. You can then identify and photocopy those articles which are of particular interest to you.

(4) Keep a reading file and regularly set aside time to read your materials. As you are likely to be otherwise preoccupied during the working day you may feel it appropriate to regularly schedule time one evening each week. Make the most of time spent travelling or waiting, for example, for a hearing at court. Anticipate when you may have free time and take two or three articles to read during that time.

(5) Learn to speed read. This technique is not appropriate for reading detailed legal documents, but it is a worthwhile technique to get through your bulk reading. Obviously you will wish to focus on certain extracts in more detail.

(6) Attendance at legal training courses is an excellent method of keeping up to date. The presenter will have spent the time researching that particular area of the law. He will have then concentrated that preparation and his knowledge into the lecture and course materials.

(7) Perhaps better still is presenting a course yourself. Volunteer to prepare a paper and present it to your department or other members of the firm.

Experience has shown that the preparation required to present a course is the best understanding the topic.

(8) One of the problems most solicitors experience is that, having spent the time reading to keep up to date, they then forget details and cannot remember where they read the particular article. You should therefore set up a system to store relevant articles. Create a filing system. Enhance that system by highlighting particularly important point in articles. Better still, write a brief note summarising the salient point in the article. By creating and maintaining this updating file you have ready access to the more important articles you have read and will be able to refer to them when appropriate.

DISASTERS — AND HOW TO AVOID THEM

As legal practice becomes more and more competitive, so the pressure is there to deal with a larger caseload and shift more work in any given hour. This can be dangerous, since rushed work leads to mistakes and potentially to negligence actions. When you first start in an office you are anxious to make a good impression, and the risk is that you volunteer to take on too much. It is a sign of strength, not weakness, to say that you already have too much on or that you are not competent to take on a particular file. As a trainee solicitor you will obviously be dealing with new matters under the supervision of your principal, so that you learn by dealing with new areas with the benefit of his experience. But the risk continues after you qualify, when you may not have so much guidance.

In the modern office, time is money, and you can minimise the risk of mistakes while maximising your efficiency by sensible use of your diary. If deadlines are meticulously noted with an advance warning that something needs to be done, if your time is carefully apportioned to allow for difficult jobs, and if your files represent a full and accurate record of the life of each transaction, things should rarely go wrong.

But, however well organised, we are all human, and we all occasionally make mistakes. If something goes wrong, don't try to hide it — eventually the client will ask what has happened. Disasters don't go away if ignored: they fester and get worse. During your articles, tell your principal immediately if something goes wrong. If you act quickly it may be possible to salvage the situation. For example, the three-year limitation period in a personal injury case can disappear very quickly. But if you notice that it has passed without a writ being issued, the court has a discretion to extend the period, depending (among other things) on the length of and reasons for the delay. The fact that you were too scared to tell anyone is not a good reason!

As a guideline of what to look out for, the following are some of the common problem areas:

PERSONAL INJURY CLAIMS

The basic three-year period runs from the date when the injury occurs, or, if later, the date when the plaintiff first knows who the defendant is and that the injury is significant. Once the writ has been issued, it must be served within four months, with the day of issue forming part of the period. Hence a writ issued on 1 January 1991 must be served by 30 April 1991, unless the court exercises its power to extend the writ.

UNFAIR DISMISSAL CLAIMS

The applicant has only three months in which to lodge an originating application. This period includes the date of dismissal.

LANDLORD AND TENANT NOTICES

Horrific problems arise with business tenancies under the Landlord and Tenant Act 1954. The most common mistake is failure to give a counter-notice within two months of receiving a statutory notice to quit. The tenant must also apply to the county court for a new tenancy within two to four months of receiving the notice to quit. If he fails to do either — or if you fail to do either on his behalf — he loses his right to claim a new tenancy. The court has no discretion to vary these periods.

CONVEYANCING

The problem here is that you are often under pressure from the client, who is always in a desperate hurry, and a lot of work is done on the phone with little time to think. Start by ensuring that you get clear initial instructions from the client, so that you know precisely what is being bought or sold and what is included or excluded. Request searches and enquiries in good time; if you are acting for the purchaser, read them, and make additional enquiries if you are not satisfied. Watch out for (e.g.) local authority charges for improvement grants, and planning proposals. If there are any encumbrances over land, give the purchaser clear written notice of them before exchange. If the property is leasehold, warn the purchaser of odd or onerous clauses and explain the effect of a full repairing covenant or a rent revision clause. If you are buying, check the property is insured from exchange. Never give an undertaking, which binds your firm, without the express authority of your principal.

POSTSCRIPT: ZEN AND THE ART OF BEING A TRAINEE SOLICITOR

Articles can be a very difficult time. You are trying hard to do things right, and to learn while also being useful. Unfortunately you are also aware of how little you know. The result is often a desperate attempt to pretend you do know what you are talking about, while being browbeaten by experienced solicitors to whom it is obvious that you are a novice. It is not always a pleasant experience, and often produces someone who is unduly submissive to qualified staff while boosting his morale by being aggressive to administrative staff. None of this is very satisfactory — for you, for your principal or for your firm.

It helps if you shift the perspective. If you accept that you are in articles to learn, that you are entitled to be unsure, then you cease to have to pretend. You have rights too, as indeed does your firm. They are entitled to expect that you should progress and become more useful, by asking for help when you need it instead of trying to save face by bluffing. So if, for example, a solicitor on the other side is trying to bully you, simply say that you do not know but you will ask your principal and ring back. This foils his attempt to make you act, probably to your client's detriment. It may also avoid an expensive mistake which really *will* make you unpopular. Similarly, clients will normally accept a simple statement that you are in training under the supervision of an experienced solicitor: they prefer this to finding the situation out later and feeling that they have been conned. Don't pretend. Accept the situation you are in. And use it positively, so that you do learn.